£ 50   AM

Rabih Hage

Quiet Architecture

DOMINIC BRADBURY

Rabih Hage
Quiet Architecture

to Basma
with my best wishes
Rabih

LUND
HUMPHRIES

First published in 2018 by Lund Humphries

Lund Humphries
Office 3, Book House
261A City Road
London EC1V 1JX
UK

www.lundhumphries.com

Rabih Hage Quiet Architecture
© Dominic Bradbury, 2018
All rights reserved

ISBN: 978-1-84822-290-8

A Cataloguing-in-Publication record for this
book is available from the British Library

Project coordinator for Rabih Hage:
William Collins
Designed by Zoë Bather
Set in Graphik and Domaine
Printed in Slovenia

Image credits
Brian Benson: 44–47, 79 / Simon Brown: 2, 7,
15, 81 (left), 96–101, 102 (below left and right),
103–105, 106 (left), 107 / Sharyn Cairns: 11,
12, 82–89, 91–95 / Sharyn Cairns / House
& Garden © The Condé Nast Publications
Ltd: 108–116, 117 (right), 118 / Didier Delmas:
58–63, 70–77 / Grant Frazer: 50 (left), 51 / Jan
Kudej: 49 / Vincent Leroux: front cover, 8, 18
(left), 24 (right), 27, 28 / Yiman Lin: 123, 124
(below left) / Tony Murray: 80, 81 (right), 120,
122 (below left), 124 (above left and right,
below right), 125 / Marcus Peel: 10, 13, 14, 18
(right), 30–43, 64–69, 117 (left), 127, 129–137,
146–159 / Marco Pinarelli: 9 / Richard Power:
17, 19, 20, 22–23, 24 (left), 25, 29, 50 (right),
52–57 / Jason Schmidt: 90 / Luke Sprague:
160 / Richard Waite: 102 (above), 106 (right).
All drawings: © Rabih Hage Ltd. 2018

QUIET ARCHITECTURE

So many of the great, pioneering modernist architects and designers of the twentieth century crossed borders. These modern masters saw few barriers between different disciplines of design, and switched constantly between architecture, interiors, furniture, lighting and other spheres. Polymaths such as Le Corbusier, Alvar Aalto, Arne Jacobsen, Gio Ponti and Ludwig Mies van der Rohe worked at a range of different scales without any inhibition upon their imaginations. Anything seemed possible.

Today, we are living in an era of increasing specialism. In the early twenty-first century, our ways of learning and working tended to push designers into very specific fields, making it harder than ever to become a successful polymath. The borders between the disciplines have, in other words, become more defined and difficult to navigate, risking a corresponding reduction in cross-fertilisation between the fields.

Rabih Hage is one of the few examples of the contemporary polymath. He is an architect but also an interior designer who designs furniture, including bespoke pieces plus his own collection, which has grown over a number of years. Hage talks as passionately about the detailing of a concealed door handle for a finely crafted wardrobe as he does about the design of a new hotel building rising among the pine trees on a Finnish island. Like so many of his own design heroes, including the modernist masters, Rabih Hage sees no reason to confine himself to one discipline alone.

Indeed, his ability to step between these different spheres of design has become one of the key points of attraction for his clients. Over time, they have come to understand and appreciate that Hage fuses architecture and interior design within one cohesive approach in which every detail is taken into account. His remit commonly extends from planning, structure and layout all the way through to the blend of furniture and art in a finely finished space. For his clients, tempted by the notion of an all-encompassing design process, this is a reassuring combination of skills that extends through many different levels within a journey to something unique and fully tailored to their own situation and aesthetic outlook. For Hage, the context of each and every project is all-important, and this includes not just the setting and surroundings but also the wishes and desires of his clients.

'I have always thought three dimensionally and in many layers', says Hage. 'Architecture does not work alone, and it's the interior design with the furniture, the art and other pieces that really bring the spaces to life. It is not only about volume and proportion but also about the softness of the interiors, the materials and the colours.

The cantilevered stone staircase at the Boltons, South Kensington, designed by Rabih Hage.

'The interesting thing for me is to have both elements in mind - architecture and interiors - so that we connect the shell and the core, the outside and the inside. It's all part of the same thought process and the same kind of thinking.'

Hage's work embraces both new-build projects and reinventions of existing buildings, with commissions in England, France, New York, Scandinavia and other parts of the world. Above all, Hage has become known for his philosophy of 'quiet architecture', with its implicit respect for the past and the intrinsic value of the architectural fabric that already exists all around us and that helps to define the places in which we live. An architect of

particular sensitivity, Rabih Hage is not an advocate of the grand statement but, rather, a passionate supporter of architectural heritage and the extraordinary stock of period buildings of all kinds that already inhabit our towns and cities.

'I have a philosophy that says why would you want to force a new form on an existing building?' says Hage. 'We have a profound respect for the gestures and decisions of other architects from the past and other lives that have been played out in these houses and buildings. So we try, wherever we can, to work with what is already there. We try to add fresh layers rather than starting all

A suspended library staircase overlooking monumental, perforated metal shutters in a Beirut penthouse.

A rustic and restored side wall at Maison Luberon, Rabih Hage's family home in Provence.

over again and we think that this is what the buildings, and their original architects, deserve.'

Rabih Hage's views about architecture and, in particular, the historical fabric of our cities were shaped by his experiences as a child and as a student. He was born in Beirut to a Franco-Lebanese family, which had long maintained close links to France. No members of his family were directly involved in architecture or design, but his father trained as an engineer and later founded a series of technical schools as well as establishing the first film festival in Beirut. There were, therefore, influences that were both creative and entrepreneurial.

As a child, Hage became fascinated with art and drawing. From around the age of five, he impressed his teachers with his drawing skills and began winning art competitions; by ten years old, he was selling some of his sketches to his school friends.

'For me, it always felt very normal to draw and sketch', Hage explains. 'I found that I could express myself through my drawing and this reinforced the idea that I wanted to do something artistic with my life. But then we had the civil war in Lebanon in the mid 1970s and, of course, it was a very upsetting time. Looking at the damage all around me, with the centre of Beirut

almost completely wiped out, I started to think as
a teenager that perhaps I should not be a sculptor or
an artist and perhaps I should be an architect instead.
It has an artistic element to it, but it would also have a
purpose in helping to rebuild. I had this in mind, even
as a child, and this is what encouraged me to start
thinking about architecture.'

Eventually, given the many dangers of staying
on in Beirut as the war continued, Hage's father took
the decision to leave. The family left their home in the
city and, after some time living in a quieter quarter of
Lebanon, decided to settle in Paris.

'Paris was the place where I felt free to discover
life and the arts on my own', says Hage. 'It already
felt familiar to me because I was bilingual and had
studied at the French lycée in Beirut, which was truly
the Paris of the Middle East with its art deco buildings
from the 1930s and avant garde modernism from the
1960s, with architecture by Alvar Aalto, Oscar Niemeyer
and others. But in Paris, I was more autonomous and
appreciated the freedom and security of the city, with
this continuous process of discovery. For me, the
transition was almost seamless and both cities are
connected in my mind somehow.

'I find it quite enriching to have this contrast
between France and the Lebanon and between these
two cultures and ways of thinking. I arrived in Paris
as a teenager and the idea, at first, was to stay there just
for the short term and then go back to Beirut. But in
the end, I was there for over twenty years. So my heart
is very much connected to France - it is my adopted
country. When I think of "home", I think of France.'

Hage was able to continue his studies, and went on
to enrol at the École des Beaux-Arts. After a foundation
course, he focused on architecture. He found the
immersive experience both 'wild and magical' - both in
terms of the teaching and the neoclassical surroundings
of the college, and its atelier system. Hage's tutors at
the Beaux-Arts, Guy Denayer and Jean Saint-Arroman,
were inspirational.

'The teaching was a mixture of major lectures,
with around two hundred students in the amazing
amphitheatres of the École des Beaux-Arts in St-Germain-
des-Prés and then collective project presentations with
some brutal corrections from the teachers and colleagues',
Hage says. 'It was wild because it was a school of survival.
Only a few of us survived all the way through and earned
our final architecture diploma. But all of us discovered
our true vocation in life, even if some left the school for
other studies and different professions. As Saint-Arroman
used to say: "architecture leads to everything that a
human wants"'.

For Hage, there was a powerful mix of this traditional Beaux-Arts teaching plus the influence of the French modernist masters such as Le Corbusier and Robert Mallet-Stevens. One of the first Parisian apartments that Hage lived in as a young man was situated on the Rue du Docteur Blanche, which is home to a number of key buildings by Mallet-Stevens. All of these influences - the modernist and the neoclassical, the architectural and the decorative, Paris and Lebanon - began to come together just as Hage started working as an architect for the first time.

'I felt in harmony with the way of life that I imagined twentieth-century architects would have led, especially those that lived and trained in Paris before me. I was surrounded by classicism but also had the example of modernism and avant garde architecture. So I began to fuse these multi-faceted influences together in my own mind and it is because of this that I developed a broad vision of a "renaissance" approach to life and work. I feel that I can design a chair, a ceramic vessel, an interior or a residential tower with no intellectual or technical restrictions. I am never intimidated by professional and creative challenges.'

Even while he was still at the Beaux-Arts, Hage was gaining practical experience working with architectural practices in Paris. He went on to work with a structural-engineering firm that collaborated on architectural projects, providing valuable expertise in 'high tech' architectural design incorporating innovative materials and building systems. Hage was part of a crossover team between the engineers on the one hand and the architects on the other, working on commissions for TGV train stations and other large infrastructure schemes.

Yet relatively early on, Hage decided that he wanted to launch his own atelier in order to set his own direction and gain creative independence. He set up a studio in Paris with two friends, taking on almost any job that came along and working for family and friends; many of these early commissions involved updating or reworking period buildings of one kind or another.

'Working on the old fabric of a building became more and more of a speciality for me', he says. 'And then I found a project in London through some friends and then another and then a third, so I thought why not open an office in London? So I sold my flat in Paris and I made the move. Very quickly, I found that I was embraced by the interior design community and soon that became just as important as the architecture. But in my own mind I have always been the architect working on interiors. It's the old continental way of looking at things. Even if you ask me to furnish a room, to me it's still a kind of architecture. It's interior architecture, working with volumes, scale, proportion and then furniture, art and all of the other layers.'

The sitting room of the Manhattan Town House is spacious enough to accommodate a grand piano.

The dining/breakfast room at the Rough Luxe Hotel, King's Cross, with bespoke trompe l'oeil wallpaper using photos by Massimo Listri and a dining table designed by Hage, made from wood reclaimed from Brighton Pier.

Houses and apartments, in particular, soon became the backbone of Hage's work before he expanded into hotel design and other kinds of projects. Residential design offers many valuable opportunities to collaborate, not only with the architects of the past but also with today's artisans and the clients themselves. Their needs are always vital considerations, with Hage seeking to create residences that reflect the personality of his clients rather than simply imposing a particular pattern of living or an aesthetic style on them. In seeking bespoke solutions, he takes special pleasure in a creative dialogue with the fresh custodians of such period buildings as well as with the buildings themselves.

Partly because, perhaps, of the destruction that he witnessed as a child in Beirut, Rabih Hage has always nurtured a special appreciation of the value of historical architecture. This appreciation has only been reinforced by his experiences of living in Paris and London, two cities with a strong architectural identity. Many of his commissions in England, France, New York and elsewhere have involved positive and imaginative responses to requests from his clients to update and reinvent eighteenth- or nineteenth-century properties for twenty-first-century living. While some architects might see this as an opportunity to sweep away the past, while stripping back and opening up a building, Hage's

approach is much more subtle and begins with a process of research and evaluation in order to understand the true character and provenance of the building itself.

'We have to remember that we are merely temporary residents of these buildings', explains Hage. 'Yes, we can leave our own traces and marks with intelligence and imagination, but we don't have the right to fundamentally alter historic houses or interfere with their existence, as long as they are well designed and part of the wider context of a neighbourhood.

'My definition of good architecture is the use of creativity to enhance and transform existing structures to fit new functionalities and modern ways of living. This is progressive architecture, which will help preserve the environment, increase energy efficiency, reduce waste and minimise impact upon the urban fabric.'

Hage is, in his own way, a champion of heritage and conservation. Yet, at the same time he is a disciple of modernism and fresh thinking. The result is the evolution of his own philosophy, 'quiet architecture', which allows space for the contemporary and the historical to coexist in harmony. Hage's work makes room for modern luxuries, amenities and services but also respects and restores period elements that lend a building its true sense of character. These include architectural staples such as volume, proportion and scale, but also features

The sitting room of the
Kensington Town House
with artwork by Jessica
Rankin, a coffee table
by David Wiseman and
lime green chauffeuse
by Hage.

details such as doors and windows, floors and ceilings, fireplaces and mouldings.

A dialogue is established between old and new, in which there is a special emphasis on patina and personality. For Hage, this is, in part, a reaction against the sanctity of minimalism and an understanding that there is beauty and charm in imperfection, the layers of time and the many traces that they leave behind.

'The whole idea of quiet architecture connects with my discovery that minimalist perfection is an impossible affair', says Hage. 'I have always been attracted by the patina of old walls and the beauty of old stone surfaces and worn fabrics that tell their stories, if we only take the time to look and think. There is beauty in imperfection, which I have always looked for, even subconsciously.'

There is a strong overlap between this concept of 'quiet architecture' and environmental awareness. Buildings and materials are recycled and repurposed rather than discarded or disposed of. Even in contexts in which Hage is invited to build from scratch, there will still be a sensitivity to the environment woven throughout the project, using locally sourced or recycled materials. Hage's architecture takes into account the need to conserve energy and resources, while his interiors seek to bring fresh life and relevance to existing pieces of furniture and family pieces rather

than discarding them in favour of the new. Such pieces combine with bespoke designs, antiques, contemporary designs and repurposed elements within a carefully considered blend of past and present, tied together by threads of colour, texture and materiality.

Hage's passion for quiet architecture has led him, inevitably, to an appreciation of other designers who adopt a similar sensibility and share his love of materials and surfaces shaped by time. These include furniture and lighting designers such as Piet Hein Eek and Stuart Haygarth, who use recycled and repurposed materials in their own work. Sometimes there is juxtaposition or purposeful contrast within Hage's spaces - between, for instance, a fine antique chair and a table made of recycled timber speckled with fading paint. This is part of the charm of his approach, which allows room for the playful and the unexpected.

The projects that follow suggest the breadth of Hage's work, from a New York town house to a Parisian apartment to a classic English rectory and an eco-hotel in Finland. Yet all could be described as examples of quiet architecture, suggesting the wide relevance and broad scope of Rabih Hage's design philosophy.

A view of the main living spaces at The Boltons, where bespoke glass and steel screens lightly divide its different zones.

Country Houses.

There is no need to wipe out an existing building to start anew just for the sake of it. Respecting the past is modernity.

– Rabih Hage

One of the downstairs
bedrooms at Hage's own
country home in France;
splashes of vivid colour stand
out against the stone walls.

Within the realm of quiet architecture, context is everything. 'Context' may refer to an existing building, or ruin, that needs to be restored and revived for twenty-first-century living with respect for its heritage and unique character. But the word also embraces the wider setting and surroundings. This includes the history and vernacular tradition of the region in question, but also - in a rural context in particular - the relationship with the landscape and the natural environment. All of these things are essential considerations for Rabih Hage when he undertakes a project, which will always begin with a careful process of research and analysis in order to better understand and appreciate the contextual framework.

'Be a good analyst and analyse your surroundings, because if you are a good analyst then you are a good architect and designer', says Hage. 'This piece of advice was given to me by one of my teachers, Guy Denayer, when I was studying architecture. Denayer worked with Le Corbusier and gave me some very valuable advice, which has stayed with me.'

Of course, the context revealed by such analysis will be unique to each project, along with the response. This, too, is a vital part of Hage's design philosophy, with each and every commission representing an opportunity to do something fresh and individual rather than repeating ideas. Hage's approach to the

design of his own home in the Luberon, Provence (see page 21) was partly determined by the provenance of the derelict seventeenth-century stone barn that he restored and converted, as well as its relationship with the gardens and the wider surroundings. His approach to the conversion of a broken-down Victorian garden building in Oxfordshire into a pool house (see page 39) was, naturally, completely different. In each case, such a sensitive and individualistic approach results in something fresh that also feels as though it truly belongs to its setting.

'This sense of belonging is very important to me', says Hage. 'With my house in France, for example, you could almost imagine that it has been this way forever even though much of it has been rebuilt and restored. It has to feel natural and to achieve this you have to recognise and appreciate the elements that give a space its own personality. With my own house, it was a process of understanding the things that I loved about the ruin when I first saw it - an odd, arched door, for example, where you had to bend down to pass through into the next room. These are the things that made me feel, yes, this is going to be my house.

'It was a similar process with the pool house in Oxfordshire. We loved the way that the plants were growing up the brick wall that formed part of the original

Victorian garden shed and this old wooden door within the wall. We made sure that we kept those elements but then you go through the door and you have this new space inside. It is about recognising the personality of the building and understanding what you have to keep hold of in order to extend this personality, while adding all that you need from the point of view of functionality. The aesthetic layer that you add on top of this should not overpower the personality that is already there. This is the recipe for a kind of quiet architecture. It is a universal recipe, in a way, but you have to begin afresh with every project.'

Hage's own house in France has become a very personal and carefully considered exemplar of quiet architecture. It was a project with which Hage was able to take his time, with the entire design and restoration process taking around ten years. Like the much-respected wines of this part of Provence, ideas were allowed time

to mature and develop. Initially, Hage concentrated on restoring the original structure of the stone building while still engaged with the process of analysing and understanding what made the barn so unique. Over time, he then began to integrate the functional aspects of the project into his plans, working out how to introduce three bedrooms, two bathrooms, a kitchen and a spacious and welcoming living room that would suit himself, his wife and their two children.

Working with local artisans and stone masons was one of the great pleasures of the project, with Hage embracing not only the luxury of time but also the opportunity to collaborate with the local craftsmen. Their own ways of working and their reactions to the building fed into the way in which the project gradually evolved.

'I really liked this way of working', he says. 'The building became almost like a sculpture with a degree of improvisation to it. Having lived in France and speaking

One of the family bedrooms at Maison Luberon, the Hage family retreat in Provence. Embroidery by Edith Mézard.

A view from the kitchen to the lower level dining room at the Old Rectory in Oxfordshire.

their language fluently, I talked to the masons with their own vocabulary and the jargon of building in this part of France, so I had the chance to adapt some of my ideas to the way that the local builders work. There should be time, within any project, to allow ideas to mature and to change your mind now and again.'

In this way, Hage was able to integrate the functional programme that he and his family needed while conserving the essence of the original barn. The craftsmanship of the artisans was in synergy with the crafted, vernacular quality of the original stone building. Hage would make sketches on site for the builders, and there would be long discussions over how to achieve the best result.

The new staircase that ties the two levels of the house together was, for instance, a subject of many conversations. The staircase needed to be relatively compact to avoid wasting valuable space, but Hage is not at all fond of spiral staircases. The solution was bespoke, consisting of a modern take on the traditional French escalier balancé in which each step twists round at an irregular angle of its own, creating a fluid, curving path.

Ultimately, Hage was able to balance the need within the barn for a sense of space and openness with the more private spaces that house the bedrooms and bathrooms. In doing so, the original spirit and personality of the barn, with its exposed stone walls, was patiently preserved.

'It was very important to me that nothing about it felt fake in any way', says Hage. 'We wanted to restore the barn and then make clear that every new addition is new. There is no pretence or pretending that something is old or authentic when it's not. The most contemporary elements are the new pergola in the garden and the swimming pool and they are very clearly modern. That is the intention and the original barn is still there, with its own personality and its own special context.'

The main living area of Hage's family home in Provence holds a dining area at one end and a seating zone around the fireplace at the other.

MAISON LUBERON

Provence, France

For many years, Rabih Hage resisted the idea of putting down roots. A long and peripatetic period of living and working between Paris and London reinforced a notion that while the buildings that we live in should last for centuries, our own time within them is often relatively brief and transient. But over time, the temptation grew to have a place that he could truly call home and that would be a permanent refuge for himself and his family. Eventually, during a visit to see a friend in the Luberon, Hage fell in love with the region and the temptation became overwhelming.

'It's a magical part of France', says Hage. 'The countryside has a warmth to it and there is beautiful light, skies and scenery in the Parc Naturel de Luberon. I said to myself that if one day I decide to own something, then it will be here. A few years later we found a barn - a ruin with a broken roof, covered with ivy, and a fig tree next to it. That was how it was, but we saw the potential to do something special.'

This marked the beginning of a ten-year project to restore the ruin, situated in a small hamlet in the Luberon, and convert the seventeenth-century barn into a family home. The project became the most personal example of Hage's commitment to 'quiet architecture', creating a contextual home that is sensitive to the natural surroundings as well as the history and character of the original stone building.

Drawing on the talents of local masons and artisans, Hage began by repairing the stonework and concentrating on restoration. Taking time to allow his ideas to mature, he developed plans that would maximise the spatial potential of the barn - which is tucked into a gentle slope - and connect it with the gardens alongside. Strict planning controls limited the possibility of an extension, so Hage worked within the parameters of the existing footprint while also seeking to ensure privacy for both himself and his new neighbours.

The main living room is on the lower level of the building. With its high ceilings and sense of openness, this multifunctional space echoes the original character of the barn, while a wall of sliding glass to one side opens on to a private courtyard. With a dining area at one end and a seating zone at the other, arranged around the bespoke fireplace, this is a light and welcoming space that spills out into the courtyard terrace during the summer months. Two bedrooms also sit on this same storey, placed to the side and rear of the central living space.

The bespoke staircase takes you to the upper level, which features a mezzanine study and lounge, overlooking the living room below, as well as to a third bedroom. The custom-designed kitchen, also positioned on this upper storey, feeds through to an outdoor living and dining room protected by a new pergola, serving as

A view of the swimming pool in the freshly landscaped gardens of Maison Luberon; the house itself sits to the left.

A custom canopy creates a pergola in the garden, lending shade to the outdoor dining area; these outdoor spaces are a key part of the house in the summer months.

a key family space during the warmer times of the year. The freshly landscaped gardens include a long, slender pool with a sculptural quality of its own.

'The only new and modern part of the house is the pergola, which is our outdoor living space', says Hage. 'The swimming pool was designed to be functional but also to feel as though it's part of the landscaping around the house. We are also planting some olive trees in the garden. The garden, which is just under a hectare, was another project in itself.'

Over the ten years that Hage worked on the house, he embraced the opportunity to work closely with the local builders and take a more organic approach than usual. It was a form of 'slow architecture' with its own delights. But after a decade, his family realised that he was, perhaps, frightened of finally calling an end to an experience that was so pleasurable and rewarding.

'In a way, I was subconsciously delaying it', Hage explains. 'I liked the idea of dreaming and extending the dream. Once you have done it all, it's there and fixed in time and space. Also, I liked this way of working with a degree of improvisation and adapting my ideas to the way that the local artisans work in this part of France.'

The choice of furniture and art is also highly personal, but very much in tune with both Hage's preoccupations and the textures and patina of the barn itself. There are many bespoke elements but also pieces by Piet Hein Eek, Patrice Gruffaz and other contemporary designers, as well as warm examples of mid-century design, such as the oval dining table by Peter Hvidt. For Hage and his family, who have seen the project grow over the years, the house now feels very much like home.

'When we left for London after spending our first summer in the house, it felt as though we were leaving a member of the family behind', says Hage. 'It's the same feeling every time. Each time we arrive back at the house it's like a big reunion. It's the first time I have had this feeling about a house. It is like falling in love or having a child. It's a relationship that you build over time.'

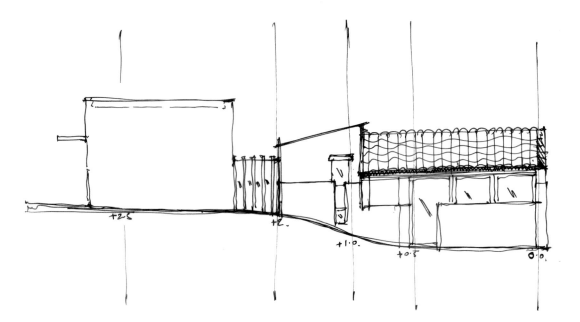

The vintage dining table
is by Peter Hvidt and the
Swedish chairs are from
the 1960s; the painting to
the right is by Aki Kuroda.
The kitchen features
bespoke cabinets; the
doorway leads out to
the verandah.

The sofa and armchairs in
the main living space are
by Piet Hein Eek.

Hand sketches showing
design development of
the house.

The courtyard alongside
the main living area
forms a more sheltered
and private outdoor room;
the furniture was made
locally using recycled
petrol cans painted to
look like silver birch.

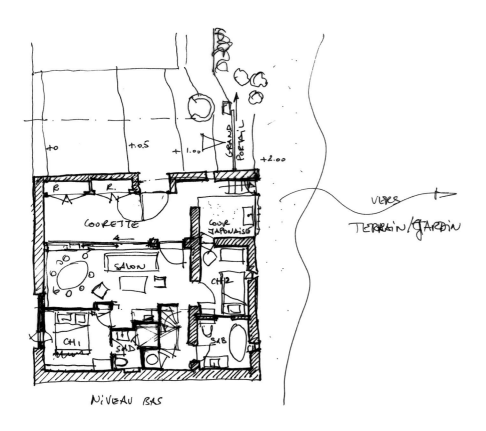

NIVEAU BAS

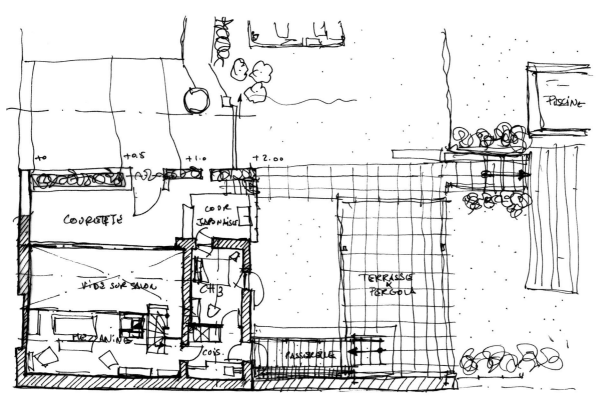

NIVEAU HAUT

A detail of the outdoor dining area, with dining table and chairs by Unopiù. Below, mezzanine with rocking chair by Rabih Hage and yellow artwork by Karen Ryan.

The master bedroom with
a bespoke headboard
designed by Rabih Hage
and soft furnishings
in vintage textiles by
Edith Mézard.

THE OLD RECTORY

Oxfordshire, UK

Situated in the heart of rural Oxfordshire, the Old Rectory is a characterful home layered with history. Parts of the building, which sits within extensive gardens close to the village church, date back to the seventeenth century, with alterations and additions from the nineteenth. This charming, listed house holds many period features including fireplaces, floors and arched windows, which needed to be both preserved and respected. At the same time, Hage and his clients - a family that he has now worked with on a number of occasions - wanted to create a weekend home that was not only welcoming but also full of interest and texture. The curation of the spaces themselves and their furnishings is eclectic, combining reverence for the building itself with a desire to step away from the formality of a traditional English country home.

'It was very much about respecting the house and the gardens, with this beautiful lawn at the back and these mature trees', says Hage, 'but we also wanted to add other layers of texture and colour, with a mix of furniture and found objects from France and Spain, as well as pieces that were already in the family. A theme that we worked with was "faded grandeur", making the most of original elements like the magnificent wooden floors and the cornicing. The staircase, for example, is seventeenth century so we didn't touch it apart from re-varnishing the woodwork. But at the same time, we wanted to bring

something fresh and make the house work for the family and the children.'

Given the protected status of the house, there were no alterations to the fabric of the main building beyond restoration and cosmetic changes. Hage fixed an eye-catching antique clock face, sourced from the Puces de St-Ouen flea market in Paris, to an exterior wall near the side entrance, adding a touch of drama and interest but without impacting upon the building itself. Hage's clients had hoped to enlarge some narrow windows around the family dining room, alongside the kitchen, but the listed status of the house prevented such changes.

'So we inserted mirrors on the shutters so that when they are open you have this impression from within of wider windows and more light', says Hage. 'You also have the reflection of the garden coming inside, so it makes the space feel larger and brighter. This is the kind of intervention that we worked with - something subtle and not too dramatic, but that makes a positive difference.'

Other changes in this part of the house include a patinated metal banister that protects the steps leading up to the kitchen, while the kitchen itself was fully updated. There are also custom-designed units and an island, which have been painted a duck-egg blue that sings out against the cream-coloured walls and rustic wooden floors.

The dining room mixes a period chandelier with a contemporary table by Piet Hein Eek.

The vintage clock on the exterior wall was found in a Paris flea market. Below, the kitchen units were updated and repainted.

In the drawing room
the painting is by Ian
McKeever and the French
sofa is in the style of Louis
XVI; the vintage chairs
are by Lee Woodard,
re-upholstered in
a linen chevron.

The dining room features
a mix of Louis XVI French
chairs and modernist
pieces by Mies van der
Rohe; the portrait is by
Hendrik Kerstens.

Textural contrasts add another key dimension throughout the home. Along with the timber and plastered walls, Hage has used fabric on the walls of a number of rooms, including the master bedroom, not just for contrast but to soften the spaces and help dampen down the acoustics. The seventeenth-century timber-panelled room on the ground floor was softened with a large Persian rug in combination with an oversized comfort chair by the fireplace and upholstered vintage rocking chairs by the windows.

The selection of art and furniture is eclectic and fresh, tied together by subtle signals such as colour, tone and texture while also allowing pieces to play with one another. The dining room is a dramatic example. This is an evening room, with the walls in a pearlescent black in order to connect with the dark hues of the stone fireplace, while an antique chandelier floats above the dining table. Among these period elements, a striking modern photograph by Hendrik Kerstens (taken of his daughter, in the style of the Dutch master painters) forms a key focal point. The furniture, too, balances contrasts and cohesion, with a Piet Hein Eek dining table bordered by both period Louis XVI-style chairs and a pair of Mies van der Rohe MR chairs in the early modernist style. The references and layers of interest are complex and considered, but the respect for the proportions of the room and its original, period features are intrinsic. Such eclecticism manages to limit the formality of the spaces themselves while also introducing both modernity and personality.

'What pleases the client most is that the house is very relaxed', Hage explains. 'Even though it is quite a grand house, it is certainly relaxing and the textures, colours and so on help to make it a place of retreat. But at the same time, it's never over the top. It's all about the balance between the old stone and the period elements with the new pieces. It's a soft touch - we didn't shake anything or force anything here. There's a new lease of life for the house but an understanding that the clients are temporary occupiers of the rectory. We will move on but the rectory, and its character, will still be there.'

Far left, Hage used inset mirrors around the door arches of the breakfast room to lend the doorways the impression of width and introduce more light. Left, Flemish-style console table in the entrance hall.

The spacious drawing room features a mix of mid-century and period French furniture.

Frank Gehry chairs
border the vintage table
on the landing.

THE POOL HOUSE

Oxfordshire, UK

Sitting within a tranquil Oxfordshire garden, this pool house is a fitting example of quiet architecture in a rural context. The original building was a derelict, nineteenth-century shed that formed one of a small collection of Victorian structures in the grounds of a country house within a quiet, rural village near Banbury. An orangery once stood alongside it, within a sheltered and private enclave that is now home to the swimming pool itself.

'The project was about restoring something that was completely broken and giving it a new life', says Hage. 'The roof of the shed was coming down, the building was damp and it was full of rubbish. We used the same shape, the existing walls, and gave this structure a new life and purpose. It feels as though it has been there for ages but there is this new functionality. It is, absolutely, quiet architecture.'

The new swimming pool is framed by Portland stone and sits at the heart of a hidden courtyard formed by a combination of the brick walls of the old shed plus hedging and a new stone wall at one end, which protects a greenhouse and vegetable garden. The pool is lined with slate that lends a greater impression of depth, yet also takes it beyond the domestic and lends the basin a more ornamental quality, working in tandem with the planting and landscaping around it. Verdant creepers and borders of agapanthus soften the Victorian walls of the

Slate was used to line the swimming pool itself, creating the sense of depth and contrasting with the lighter stone of the terrace.

pool house, with a single, subtle door in the brick façade offering an understated and enigmatic entrance to the building that sits in tune with its original provenance.

Hage restored the fabric of the former shed, installing skylights in the roof and digging down to slightly lower the floors, which are also coated in Portland stone and feature underfloor heating. The brick walls are left exposed, with Hage keen to retain the remnants of faded paint upon the brick, while the ceiling beams are also clear to see. In this way, the historical character of the structure remains open and apparent, becoming a key part of the identity of the pool house.

'We renovated the walls, but I used to go down on site once a week to stop the builders cleaning the brickwork too much', Hage says. 'We re-used the timber for the roof and repaired the original door. We wanted to keep the patina in place as much as we could.'

Beyond this, Hage took inspiration from stable buildings and other rustic structures. Bespoke and partial enclosures, rather like equine stalls, create changing cubicles that offer members of the family a degree of privacy without disturbing the overall proportions and open feel of the space. Other fitted, custom-designed elements include the vanity/storage unit.

A simple, draw-across curtain can section off an exercise room at one end, with tatami mats on the floor

Mechanical pumps and
services for the pool are
hidden under the tatami
mats and floor; the curtain
to this exercise space
can be drawn across
for privacy.

The design of the changing cubicles takes inspiration from Victorian stables, while the brickwork was left purposefully exposed with the remnants of old paintwork preserved for its patina.

The pool itself has an
enigmatic quality, both
functional and ornamental
in the manner of a water
feature; climbers soften
the restored brickwork.

and fitted storage benches against the walls; the pump and other mechanical systems for the pool are hidden beneath the floor here. Lighting and other touches play with contrasts between function and ornament, with a sequence of industrial-style lights and wall lights juxtaposed with crystal chandeliers. Similarly, there are functional mirrors but also a much more ornate mirror mounted on one wall of the exercise room that was made with a repurposed, carved eighteenth-century frame sourced in the Paris flea markets. Such touches help to prevent a family space becoming too serious in character or too minimal, creating another layer of personality within the pool house.

'Almost everything here has been custom made for the project - the wall lights, the benches, the vanity unit, the tatami mats', says Hage. 'But at the same time there were a lot of things here already and in the grounds that we did not want to disturb. So everything has been done with a lot of subtlety to make sure that we maintained the beauty of the gardens.'

HOLIDAY
HOME

The Lakes By Yoo, Cotswolds, UK

The creation and curation of a second home offers a refreshing degree of freedom. Vacation and weekend houses are, by their very nature, escapes that are free from some of the everyday demands and considerations of urban living. More than this, they provide opportunities for indulgence and personal expression without some of the constraints and reservations that often temper hard-working town houses, which may be more formal on the one hand and somewhat compromised in terms of space, light and indoor-outdoor connectivity on the other.

Rural escapes offer an invitation to do things differently, and to take a more casual and free-spirited approach to design and decoration. This is very much true of this weekend and holiday home in the Cotswolds, which sits within The Lakes by Yoo, an estate with its own spa and other communal facilities. Arranged around six freshwater lakes and woodland, the houses here are designed with terraces and outside spaces that help to reinforce a strong sense of connection with the surroundings and with nature itself. Here, Rabih Hage was asked by his clients to curate the interiors of an existing waterside home designed by the Yoo 'family' of designers, which includes Philippe Starck.

'It was basically a blank canvas', says Hage. 'The clients had a good collection of art and wanted me to

work with their collection and furnish the house in style. But they also wanted furniture, lighting and other pieces that have meaning and would keep their value. So we were very much working on this project as curators more than anything, making sure that we had the right pieces for the right space. The clients are a family of four with a house in London, so this was about creating a weekend getaway that would be warm and welcoming.'

One key element of the project was lighting. Hage decided on a number of statement designs that stand out vividly against the neutral backdrop of walls and pale-timber floors. A key choice was Stuart Haygarth's Tail Light - a chandelier made with repurposed car- and other vehicle-light casings - which sits over the dining table in the double-height atrium at the heart of the building. Innovative and original, Haygarth's work has climbed in value along with other pieces curated for the house.

These include the sculptural, sinuous coin sofa by American designer and artist Johnny Swing that forms a focal point in the sitting room, made with a coat of shimmering, circular coins. Hage has supported Swing's work for many years, and the piece sits well alongside the centre table in the sitting room by Hubert le Gall, complemented by sink-in sofas and armchairs.

The house features a number of designs by the Dutch furniture designer and maker Piet Hein Eek, including the

A double-height space at the centre of the house hosts the dining area, with a chandelier by Stuart Haygarth.

The bunk beds in one of the children's bedrooms are by Piet Hein Eek.

Far left, first floor family room with an armchair and bench by Rabih Hage. Left, the dressing area/study features a bucket chair by Hage with silk screened fabric on the back by artist Susan Shup.

The statement sofa, made of coins, is by Johnny Swing; the central table is by Hubert le Gall.

tall cabinet in the central atrium and bunk beds for one of the children's bedrooms, as well as chairs and other pieces. Eek uses recycled timber in his furniture, which has the character of 'rough luxe' that fascinates Hage and threads through his own approach to design. Hage has worked with Eek for many years, staging London exhibitions of his work, commissioning bespoke designs for interiors projects and including his furniture within his own family homes in London and Provence.

'I first went to see Piet Hein Eek in Holland thinking he was a one man band working from his garage', says Hage. 'I found out that he had a handful of passionate people working with him in a small workshop and a good reputation in Holland already, but that he was almost unknown internationally. Now he has dozens of people working with him and a massive workshop. There is beauty in imperfection and I have always been attracted by designs and sculptural objects made out of discarded materials. At an early age I was a big admirer of sculptor

Jean Tinguely, who used recycled mechanical elements in his work, and I see the similar kind of ethos in the designs and artworks of Johnny Swing and Piet Hein Eek.'

Such textures and patina add a significant layer of interest and fascination within the cabin, helping to lift the spaces in combination with the clients' paintings. Textiles also help to add texture and soften the spaces throughout, with a selection of rugs as well as upholstered pieces and diaphanous silk and linen curtains. There is an open warmth to the spaces, reinforced by the rural setting, and a balance between the open volume of the atrium and more intimately scaled areas, with lower ceilings, such as the sitting room.

'When it's a house in the countryside, a second home, then the client has already done everything once with their main residence', says Hage. 'So in the country they can really relax and their true personality can come out. My job is to listen to that and to transcribe it in objects and materials.'

Pieds-à-Terre. Creating functionality within spaces is easy but hiding it effortlessly should be the objective of every designer.

– Rabih Hage

Reception and gallery
space at The Chilterns
in Marylebone, London.
Lighting installation by Hage
in collaboration with Lasvit.

The design of a successful and welcoming pied-à-terre offers many challenges. These are, generally, compact homes at the heart of the city where space is at a premium. Pieds-à-terre have to work hard, combining multiple functions and meeting many different needs, with each and every corner of the home put to good use.

Central urban apartments have many advantages, of course. They offer the varied pleasures of living at the thriving core of a great city such as Paris or London. The journey to work becomes more manageable, freeing up time and promoting well-being in comparison to a long and stressful commute from the suburbs or beyond.

These were key considerations for Rabih Hage when he first settled in London. Early on, he decided that he wanted to live centrally and be able to walk to his atelier each day; for 14 years he did not own a car. Today, he and his family still live centrally and the architect spends perhaps 15 minutes walking to his atelier near Sloane Square each day.

The decision to live so centrally implies, for most, certain compromises in the scope and scale of the pied-à-terre itself. Having started with a small apartment, Hage and his family now live in a quiet mews house (see page 53), which is modestly scaled but also calm and delightful. For vacations and quieter times of the year, the family travel to their home in Provence (see page 21), where - in

contrast - the context is rural with a spacious garden, and there is an open invitation to escape into nature and enjoy a very different way of life. These are the kind of trade-offs and arrangements that often evolve around the idea of a pied-à-terre, with juxtapositions between urban life and country living.

Hage begins, as always, with a process of research in the hope of understanding what everyday functions the apartment - and the spaces within it - need to accommodate. Over the course of many conversations, the requirements of the clients become clear. These needs can, of course, be very different according to individual situations - and the programme of a bachelor, for instance, will differ from that of a young family.

'I always design a room based upon its functions rather than a name such as "the kitchen" or "the dining room"', says Hage. 'With pieds-à-terre, especially, a room may need to cater for more than one function at the same time while the layout also needs to allow room for evolution and change, especially if there are children who will also grow and change. So we begin with a list of functions, which may overlap, and then we start to sculpt the space.'

Yet the common necessity to combine different functions in one space does not lead, in Hage's approach, to open-plan living or a process of stripping away walls and partitions in favour of 'one-hit' living spaces. Such an approach has become increasingly commonplace - particularly for apartments aimed at a younger audience and those who want a more informal, casual, studio-style way of living.

'Having a big open space works for a certain bracket in terms of age and lifestyle', says Hage, 'but if you have a family that is evolving then you have to include all kinds of different functions in one dwelling and make sure that it can evolve and offer longevity. Instead of being monophonic, with an open space suited to one way of life, it's about being polyphonic where you have different spaces suited to plenty of different uses over time.'

Such an approach includes a recognition of the important balance between 'public' and 'private' space. Flexible and fluid spaces, such as a spacious kitchen, may allow all sorts of family activities to take place in one room - cooking, eating, homework, playing or listening to music and so on. A dining room might double as a study and family lounge, as with the apartment that Hage designed in London's Palace Gate (see page 59). A large sitting room may offer space and opportunity for a dining table, as

seen in the Paris apartment in the Trocadéro district of the city (see page 71). But Hage also pays close attention within such homes to the creation of more intimate, private retreats including bedrooms and study spaces. The opportunity to step back and enjoy a degree of solitude and calm, at times, is a key part of the overall design approach even within the constraints of a pied-à-terre.

'Within families, especially, you don't really want to spend every moment with the rest of your family next to you, however close you are', Hage says. 'Every now and again you want to go off and escape, enjoying your own time in your own space. The important thing is to have a choice and if there is just one big open space then you haven't got many choices.'

Hage and his atelier have also completed successful commissions for new apartment buildings that also include reception spaces and other key communal areas, which play a vital part in establishing the identity and character of the residential development itself. At The Chilterns in London's Marylebone, for example, Hage not only worked on designs for the interiors of the 44 pieds-à-terre in the building but also created a substantial and

The central atrium at Carlow House in London, a residential conversion by Rabih Hage of an art deco building.

Right, the welcoming roof terrace at Rabih Hage's mews house in central London.

spacious reception zone that doubles as an art gallery, while other communal amenity spaces include a gym, spa and private cinema.

'The art installed in the lobby is temporary until the apartment owners get together as a "curatorial committee" and decide to put on their own shows and collaborate with young artists and photographers', explains Hage. 'For our first show the developer commissioned David Bailey to create 44 unique photographs for the gallery, which will eventually be given to the residents themselves. It helps to give the building a true pedigree but also give the lobby an authentic and additional purpose and means that the occupiers have a say in how it evolves as a collaborative communal space.'

Similarly, at Carlow House in Camden, north London, Hage was asked to work on the conversion of a landmark art deco building that included the design of vibrant communal elements and amenities. The building was adapted from offices to residential use, and a key part of the project was the creation of a dramatic atrium space sheltered under a glass roof. New balconies and internal windows look down into this centrepiece, which Hage

designed as an indoor garden complete with planters suspended from the balconies and layers of planting at ground level, interspersed with seating areas.

'There were minimal interventions to the art deco façade but inside the building we created these floating walkways that connect all of the apartments on each level and also open to the internal garden space, which is covered with a ventilated glass roof', Hage says. 'So the project was about the adaptive reuse of the building but also creating this new indoor garden for the residents. Again, like the gallery in The Chilterns, it gives this communal space another function and purpose and helps to define the building. In every project that I do there is always a sense of purpose and a considered justification for design decisions and the aesthetic. So I am very proud of these apartment projects as they relate to my conviction of how we should design with existing elements and quietly, with minimal interventions that create a strong personality.'

A sitting room at The Chilterns, arranged around a custom fireplace framed by bookshelves.

MEWS HOUSE

Chelsea, London, UK

For a number of years, Rabih Hage shuttled between Paris and London. It was the period after completing his studies in architecture, and he had projects in both cities. He first launched his atelier in France but soon found that he had more work in England. Although he still considers France his true home, Hage eventually made the decision to base himself in London, settling in Chelsea. He began with a small apartment, off the King's Road, and opened a new office a short walk away.

Although Hage has now been working and living in London for two decades, he has always kept both his home and studio in Chelsea, ensuring that the two spaces are within walking distance of one another. Now that Hage has a wife, Ghada, and two children - as well as an atelier to run - he has finally succumbed to the pressure to own a car and has also accepted the need for more living space for the family, gradually moving up the residential scale in terms of square footage. Most recently, Hage and his family moved into a pied-à-terre contained within the upper levels of a Victorian mews house.

'We have always loved this area and it has become our village in London', says Hage. 'We all like the neighbourhood and we have many connections here. The mews itself is on a quiet, calm street but it is also very central, and I can still walk to work. I much prefer the arrangement to the idea of a long commute.'

Hage and his family were drawn to the mews house not only due to its familiar position within the geography of London, but also by the spaces and volumes inside it. The house features a spacious living and dining room leading out to a secluded roof terrace, which becomes a much-used outdoor room in the summer months - a secret garden, used for both dining and relaxing in the fresh air. There is also a substantial family kitchen with plenty of space for a more informal dining area at one end, with the table itself - designed by Hage - doubling as a desk for homework and sketching ideas.

The greatest challenge lay in navigating the narrow entrance and staircase up to the family quarters, which required some imagination in terms of introducing furniture of manageable proportions. Even so, the mews house served as a suitable and light 'canvas' for many pieces of Hage's own design. These include a number of creations from his own furniture collection, such as a steel-and-glass coffee table in the living room, as well as the sofa and the limed oak bench. There are also bespoke elements such as the bookshelf by the formal dining table (also designed by Hage), which had to come in section by section.

'I designed the collection on my train trips between London, Paris and Brussels, where my manufacturer is based', says Hage. 'The coffee table, for instance, is made

In the main seating area, the sofa is a design by Rabih Hage, the Jar Chair is by Johnny Swing, the ceramic pieces are by Carol McNicoll and the carved wood panels are by Zoé Ouvrier.

The coffee table made of steel I-beams and glass is by Rabih Hage; the rug is Nepalese by Denis Colomb.

The dining area features a table by Rabih Hage and a mix of dining chairs, including four by Romeo Sozzi.

A corner detail in the main living space shows a steel cabinet by Piet Hein Eek, coated in vintage wallpaper; the green vase is by Tord Boontje and Emma Woffenden and the 3D-printed rocking antelope is by Michaella Janse van Vuuren.

with a steel I-beam cut into small pieces, which becomes the base, and then a glass top. A number of the designs do consist of a number of smaller pieces that combine together. Perhaps it's the influence of my nomadic past. Many of the other pieces of furniture and art are things that I have collected over the past twenty years and each of them has a story.'

There are a number of designs by Piet Hein Eek, including a large cabinet in the kitchen and the beds in the children's rooms, and a favourite chair by Johnny Swing, pieces by Patrice Gruffaz, and sculptures and

paintings gathered over the course of many trips and travels. But there is also room here for 'rough luxe' pieces, such as the Parisian flea-market table on the terrace accompanied by stools and a chair by Eek.

The mews house is certainly a family home, yet Hage still considers it to be a 'pied-à-terre' with a temporary quality to it. Having moved around Paris and London many times over, Hage happily embraces the notion of the pied-à-terre, with its particular character and purpose - particularly within a part of London that he has come to love.

The kitchen features a
cabinet and dining chairs
by Piet Hein Eek; the
breakfast table is by Rabih
Hage and works on paper
are by Susan Shup.

In the master bedroom
there is just space enough
by the window for a
console desk designed
by Piet Hein Eek.

PALACE GATE

Kensington, London, UK

'Lateral living' has many advantages. Spaces flow together without the interruption of a staircase and landings, allowing for greater connectivity and social interaction - particularly within a family home. These were important considerations when it came to the layout of this substantial apartment in central London, arranged all on one level. At one point, the family considered selling the apartment, which had become somewhat tired, but they came to recognise the value of lateral living and the generous proportions of the spaces that they already had. So, instead, they asked Rabih Hage to redesign and refresh the interiors of their home.

The redesign offered two key challenges. One was to soften the interiors to make them more welcoming, layered and suitable for family living. The second was to make the most of large, well-proportioned rooms without carving them up or introducing partitions that would undermine their character and the flow of natural light from the large windows of a building dating back to the early twentieth century.

'I wanted to bring the space alive with a discreet opulence', says Hage. 'We wanted to create rooms that were luxurious and allow the clients to present artworks that we found together. So we worked on refining the purpose of every room, defining spaces within them and giving every member of the family the bedroom that they wanted.'

Hage's response to the brief demanded a light but intelligent touch. The architect used a combination of methods to zone key parts of the apartment, such as the main living room. Here a custom-made, hand-woven rug sitting on the parquet floor helps to demarcate the main seating area around the fireplace, in combination with Hage's art deco-influenced Bucket sofas and two armchairs covered in pony hide. An area by the bay window becomes another seating zone, with a chaise longue that serves as a reading chair oriented to connect with a key view of the leafy Kensington streetscape. A tall, bespoke mirror leaning against the wall nearby helps to further define this reading area and push light through the space. The room has been further softened with soothing colours, a paint effect for the wall that lends texture and the flowing curtains in Jim Thompson silk.

A parallel process takes place in the dining room. Here, Hage and his clients decided that devoting the entire space to a formal dining area that was seldom used made little sense in the context of a family pied-à-terre. The room was lightly zoned into two parts, again using handmade Nepalese rugs to help define the two areas in question.

By the window, Hage placed a square dining table and chairs of his own design, with a Baccarat chandelier hovering above, reinforcing the identity of this part of

In the dining room, the table is a design by Rabih Hage, while the chandelier is from Baccarat, the painting is by François Bard and the white PVC vases/lights are by Paul Cocksedge.

The sitting room features a pair of Bucket sofas by Rabih Hage, with an art deco influence, and armchairs covered in pony hide.

As is his usual process, Hage developed the layouts, in this case of furniture, by hand sketch.

The vibrant artwork by Aki Kuroda shines out against the neutral colour palette of the walls with a linen paint effect by Croxford and Saunders.

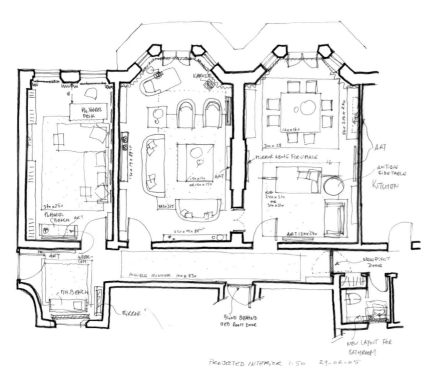

the room. The table doubles as a work space or study for the children, where homework can be supervised by the parents if needed.

The other part of the room has now become a casual and more inviting family lounge, with comfortable seating, a coffee table and soft lighting that enhances the soothing, green-grey colours of the walls and fabrics. For entertaining, the lounge also serves as a kind of anteroom for conversation and drinks before moving across to the dining table. In this way, the room serves many uses and becomes a space that is used by the family every day rather than just on special occasions.

Elsewhere, Hage paid close attention to the entrance hall and the long circulation corridor. The hallway became more welcoming, with rugs and seating as well as artworks and tall mirrors. The long corridor was interrupted with a new and tall wooden door, which help to divide the 'public' and private portions of the apartment.

As well as many pieces of Hage's own design, there are also elements within the mix from other designers and artists. There is the coffee table in the sitting room by Mark Harvey, for example, and a striking collection of sculpted lights in the dining room/lounge by designer Paul Cocksedge.

'Most of the colours for the walls and upholstery are neutral and soothing', says Hage, 'so the bursts of colour and interest from the artworks, glassware and ceramics can speak for themselves and add another layer of personality. That's what this apartment is all about.'

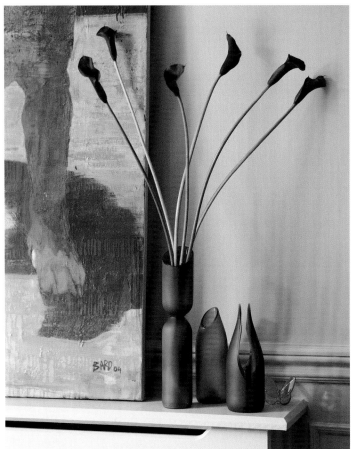

Texture is a key aspect of the interior treatment, expressed in a variety of finishes and details.

This part of the dining room has been adapted into a lounge, creating a secondary use for a space that was once seldom used. Painting by Susan Shup, coffee table by Mark Harvey and rug, as in all rooms, by Hage.

PRINCE'S GATE COURT

South Kensington, London, UK

Over recent years, the push towards informal, multifunctional living spaces has seen many period houses and apartments taken in the direction of open-plan living. Walls are taken down, rooms opened up and connected with one another to create more fluid and free-flowing spaces within the contemporary home. Yet such connectivity does not always work so well, especially when the resulting spaces become 'prairie rooms' with an uneasy scale and difficult proportions. Rabih Hage found just such a space within a client's flat in a 1940s' apartment building in South Kensington.

The apartment was dominated by a long, open living room with relatively low ceilings and no sense of welcome. The client, a bachelor businessman using the apartment as his London pied-à-terre, seldom used this pivotal space and would drift away to the kitchen or another part of the home. The original apartment had been designed for 'luxury' living, yet the spaces were flawed when it came to a single resident who wanted rooms to escape within and feel a true sense of comfort.

'The client wanted to change everything at first and that was his brief', says Hage. 'But then we started looking at his furniture, the art and the things that he had, and he liked everything, because every piece had a memory or a story attached to it. So we swung round to thinking "let's keep everything" and revive the spaces themselves.'

Hage began with the prairie room, which formed the main reception area just off the entrance hall and clearly presented the greatest challenge. He looked at ways of influencing the proportions of the space and its functions with quiet interventions that would not affect the overall fabric or structure of the building. The two key interventions were a new oak architrave with panelling that helps to partially infill the wall between the hall and the living space beyond, subtly reducing the perception of open space. The second step was to design and build a tall, oak bookcase that divides the room into two parts, but with space enough to either side of the bookcase to pass by and a clear gap between the top of it and the ceiling.

The bookcase becomes a crafted monolith, floating in the room, with one side devoted to books. This end of the former prairie room now serves as a welcoming library, with a chaise longue and re-upholstered easy chair that help to create the idea of a masculine retreat. The other side of the monolith offers an extra display surface for the client's extensive collection of art and photography, while this part of the overall space now serves as a dining area complete with a dining table and chairs designed by Hage in a style that has something of a refined art deco influence.

'The client loves books and likes to read a lot, so the idea was to create this comfortable reading room for him',

The monolithic bookcase acts as a partial partition between the dining area and library; the dining table and chairs are Rabih Hage designs.

The cabinet in the master bedroom is by Piet Hein Eek, sitting next to a standing mirror by Rabih Hage.

A chair by Rabih Hage in the guest bedroom has been covered in textural burlap; the artwork is by Frank Thiel.

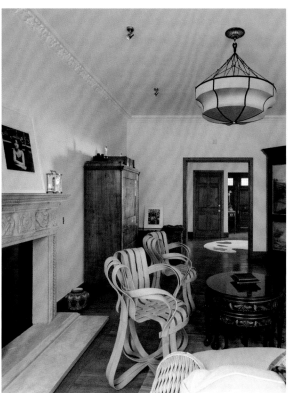

Left, the library with artwork by Calmen and Bech. Right, the sculptural chairs in the sitting room are by Frank Gehry.

says Hage. 'But apart from the shelf and the dining table most of the other pieces are things that he already had, and we re-upholstered the sofa and some armchairs. So from this big, open space we sub-divided it into these smaller spaces to make them cosier and more functional.'

Hage commissioned a number of rugs that also helped to soften key parts of the apartment, including the master bedroom. Within the guest bedroom, Hage used a tactile wallpaper to add texture - aiming, once again, to soften the interior. Here, also, there is one of Hage's own armchairs covered in a recycled burlap for contrast between the lacquered wood of the frame and the 'rough luxe' nature of the seat.

A secondary lounge hosts pieces from the client's photographic collection but also an eclectic mix of furniture. There is a pair of Cross Check plywood armchairs by Frank Gehry for Knoll, a sink-in sofa and period pieces such as the painted corner cabinet, while an ornate fireplace forms a focal point. Such pieces have been woven into the refreshed interiors, adding to the character of the home and truly reflecting the owner's personality and taste.

The custom-made bookcase helps differentiate the library from the dining area; the hallway is in the background.

PARIS APARTMENT

Trocadéro, Paris, France

Having lived, worked and studied in Paris for many years, it is a city that Rabih Hage knows intimately. He is, naturally, very familiar with the capital's stock of Haussmann-era apartment buildings and the beautifully proportioned spaces within them created during the 'reign' of Napoleon III's ambitious city planner, Baron Georges-Eugène Haussmann. These offer delightfully characterful homes, with panelled walls, plaster mouldings, ornate fireplaces and timber floors. A good friend, whom Hage has known since he was a teenager, acquired one of these apartments and asked the architect and designer to help reconfigure and update the apartment for herself and her family.

'The clients lived in Japan and China for many years before returning to France and buying this apartment', says Hage. 'So this was, in a way, their final stop and they brought a number of pieces with them from Asia - furniture, art and decorative panels - and these became an important ingredient within the interiors.'

The flat sits on the fourth floor of a building in the Trocadéro - a very central portion of Paris, close to the Seine, where the Trocadéro Gardens sit opposite the Quai Branly. The front of the apartment and its reception rooms face a picturesque street and the rear overlooks a courtyard, with generously sized windows introducing plenty of light.

Hage adjusted the layout of the apartment to help create a more spacious master suite, which took the place of one of the old reception rooms, as well as creating a larger family kitchen. Original elements, such as the cornicing and parquet floors, were preserved and restored with respect for the provenance of the building.

Having established a floor plan better suited to the needs of the family, Hage began to develop the interiors with a subtle East-meets-West influence inspired by his clients' Asian travels and the pieces that they had brought back with them.

The floor-to-ceiling windows combined with high ceilings and grand proportions in the main living room, provide a delightful canvas. Here, Hage picked upon a soothing light-grey colour for the panelled walls, with the colour reaching from the floor right up to the cornices. Repeated lilac tones and highlights sit well against the soft greys, as well as representing a favourite colour for the clients. Variations of lilac and soft purple reappear in the upholstery, light shades and other elements within the room.

Asian influences include the handmade silk rug, with a Japanese-inspired pattern; Chinese and Japanese cabinets either side of the fireplace; and Jim Thompson Thai silks for the curtains. Beyond this, the choice of seating around the fireplace is eclectic with a comfortable

The main seating area is arranged around the original fireplace, with lilac tones in the fabrics and lighting standing out against the greys and white of the walls and ceiling.

The apartment offers constant contrasts between dark and light, as seen in this glimpse of the master bedroom.

A Marcel Wanders Skygarden light floats over the breakfast table off the kitchen, which is enclosed by the curved red lacquered doors.

The combined dining area and sitting room features a soft palette of greys and lilac tones; the antique wall panel is Japanese.

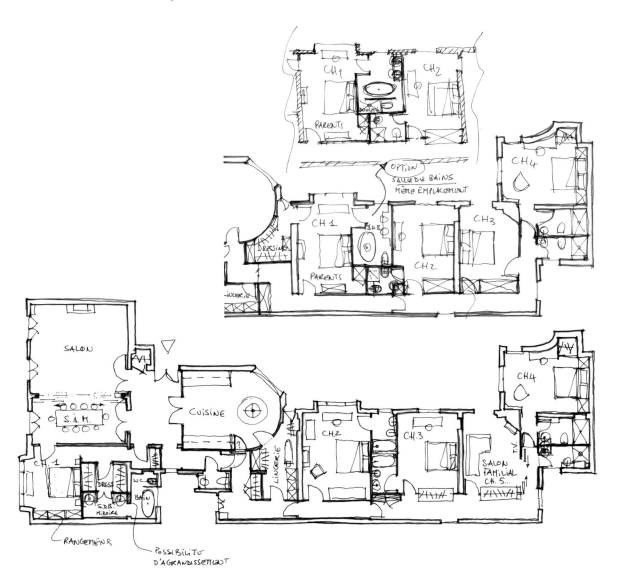

Chesterfield sofa, re-upholstered antique Louis XV French armchairs and a contemporary coffee table by Christian Liaigre. Other small but playful touches, such as the wall lights either side of the fireplace by Patrice Gruffaz and Ingo Maurer, prevent the space becoming overly serious. At the other end of the room, Hage created a formal dining area for entertaining. Here, too, there is a similar blend of elements and references, with a dining table by Cassina, bespoke dining chairs and a Japanese wall-mounted panel with sconces by Gruffaz and Maurer to either side.

The design of the enlarged kitchen was tailored to the needs of a young family. This is now a multifaceted space with a family dining table - overseen by a Marcel Wanders Skygarden pendant light - serving as a crucial everyday hub. There is also space for a piano nearby, while a floating island serves as the more formal part of the kitchen; a pantry and prep area sits behind lacquered sliding doors, which also have something of a Japanese flavour.

There is a somewhat similar combination of greys and vivid highlights in the entrance hall, with its pebble-like Koishi pouf by Naoto Fukasawa for Driade, made in vibrant orange fibreglass. Elsewhere, there are little gestures towards traditional French interiors, as with the toile de jouy wallpaper in the cloakroom.

More than anything, it was the collaborative nature of this project that pleased Hage the most and the way in which the apartment truly reflects the personality of its owners as well as showing some reverence towards its own history.

'Sometimes people get lost in ideas when they are working on their home but not here', he says. 'What's great about this apartment is that it is unique because it is about them as a family. It was really my job to listen to them and echo who they are and bring in these pieces that they love, from Japan and from their travels. So it is very different to anything else but it never feels staged. For them, it's all very natural as any home should be.'

A Japanese Tansu cabinet sits to the left of the fireplace, while the seating mixes restored Louis XV armchairs with a Chesterfield sofa.

Red is a repeated theme throughout, seen within a series of high notes that stand out against a subtle backdrop. The armchair is an iconic design by Gerrit Rietveld.

Left, in the main living room an artwork by Aki Kuroda stands out against the grey walls; the curtains are in Jim Thompson Thai silk and the armchairs were designed for the client with bespoke gaufrage velvet to the backs.

Opposite, subtle fluctuations in texture and tone create cohesive but layered spaces. The bespoke bronze bedside table designed by Hage was inspired by a Brâncuşi sculpture.

Town Houses.

A house might be a machine for living yet the balance between voids and solids is the poetry that makes it sing.

– Rabih Hage

Bespoke glass and steel decorative gates by Christophe Côme in a Holland Park residence. Large lighting installation and dining chairs by Rabih Hage.

The character of a city is formed of many layers. Over time, cities change and evolve yet somehow manage to retain a character rooted in history, patterns of living and shifting architectural traditions. These layers intertwine and overlap, all adding to a complex tapestry. This urban fabric makes room for change and modernity, yet the way in which we think of a city is often rooted in dominant styles and periods of architecture that have become essential points of reference within the overall pattern of development.

To think of London is to think of Georgian houses and Victorian terraces as much as modern skyscrapers. Conjuring a picture of Paris might well include reference to the countless apartment buildings and *hôtel particuliers* developed in the nineteenth century under the watch of prefect and master planner Georges-Eugène - or 'Baron' - Haussmann. New York is still defined, in part, by its many rows of brownstone houses. The old towns (or medinas) of North African cities such as Marrakech and Fez are dominated by their historic riads and dars - arranged around, respectively, their central gardens or courtyards.

In each case, it is true that a distinctive and endearing version of the town house plays a crucial part in forging the identity of a city. Town houses are an essential part of the building stock, but also bring with them a key component of the visual personality, of an urban quarter. When they are broken up into apartments

or perhaps replaced by towering apartment buildings, there are - inevitably - shifts and changes in the make-up of the neighbourhood itself, for better or for worse. Many planning authorities now protect historic town houses as a heritage asset, recognising their value not simply as a place to live but also as a component part of the unique identity of an urban 'village'.

The philosophy of 'quiet architecture' developed by architect Rabih Hage incorporates a profound respect for the town house and other characterful, period buildings within the cityscape. For Hage, the notion of 'urban renewal' encapsulates sensitivity towards such buildings with the aim of preservation and enhancement rather than replacement.

'A town house is anchored in its surroundings', says Hage. 'It is such an important part of a neighbourhood but it is also shaped by its neighbourhood. Each one is an individual personality within the streetscape or mini urban village. We are merely temporary occupiers of these buildings. We represent one of the many layers of occupation within the existence of the town house and we should respect this, as well as the importance of the layers left behind by the residents before us. It's all part of the narrative of the location.'

As an architect, Hage approaches any intervention with a light and respectful touch. His town house commissions involve challenges focused upon a demand for modern services and ways of accommodating twenty-first-century patterns of living, which are generally more fluid and informal than they were in the past. Yet the historic proportions, scale and period features of town house spaces are, for Hage, characterful elements that demand the utmost respect.

For instance, Hage talks of the particular importance of window patterns and design, as seen from both within and outside. The fenestration of a period house forms a key part of its architectural identity as seen from the street, with the detailing around the windows also indicative of its period and provenance. But at the same time the shutters, sashes, window bars and surrounds of the window as seen from the interior are a vital and delightful part of a period room.

'The windows frame a view and the interior becomes an ornament to that frame', says Hage. 'The verticality of period town house windows brings drama, which I play with by adding either very simple curtains or no curtains at all to accentuate their shape and form without overpowering them. These windows are just as important as the art upon the walls. Horizontal windows, on the other hand, are usually a sign of modernism and - most of the time - more dramatic in their form when seen from the outside.'

The clients who commissioned Hage to work on their New York town house - in collaboration with American architect Tom Kundig - were initially drawn to the period building by its tall and alluring, arched windows. Hage was careful to preserve and enhance the shape of these windows within the design of the corresponding spaces. The deep arches become graphic elements within the space, with no curtains to interrupt their outline. The sinuous, rounded silhouettes help to soften the interiors and work well in combination with the fluid, sculpted shape of the reinvented central staircase, which serves as a key focal point within the house as a whole.

'What I enjoy most about working on the design of a town house is the process of moulding space', Hage explains. 'It's like working on a giant sculpture and discovering new emotions every day. These residences have to be functional, but I also try to make them poetic and introduce personality, colour and a subtle degree of

The drawing room at the St John's Wood residence in London, with twin seating areas at either end of this generously scaled space.

luxury. It's important to add colour, texture and layering that corresponds to the clients' personality in a truthful way. That was very much the case in the New York house. The clients' personalities are there to see, in the art, the furniture and the style of the house.'

In some cases, there is a demand for additional living space and for modern amenities and services – including, perhaps, a swimming pool, home cinema or wine cellar. A commission in West Kensington, London, centred on a Victorian town house, presented exactly this kind of challenge (see page 109). Hage was able to create a new basement level, including a gym and cinema room, while also incorporating a new lift to one side of the property. Yet other parts of the house, particularly the main salon on the *piano nobile*, were carefully restored and many period elements reinstated.

Similarly, with a town house project in The Boltons, South Kensington, Hage extended downwards (see page 97). In this instance, the house had been divided up into two maisonettes during its long history and many period features had been lost. As well as lending character and

cohesion to the revived interiors as he put the house back together again, Hage also created three new sub-levels. These provided space for underground parking and a substantial swimming pool. Such additions added many contemporary luxuries, yet the period exterior of the house was also revived in a sensitive and contextual manner. In this way, the town house was given fresh purpose as a family home yet its period presence on the streetscape was preserved and restored.

Many town house commissions involve such careful balancing acts between introducing additional space and services while also respecting and enhancing the personality of the building itself. For Hage and his clients, these projects are responses to the beauty and history of the original architecture. They are, in a sense, acts of urban revival that give these buildings fresh relevance as twenty-first-century family homes while also protecting the special character of our urban villages.

The glazed wine cellar looks through to the dining room in The Boltons with table and chairs by Rabih Hage and chandelier by Ingo Maurer.

The entrance hall and stairway of the St John's Wood town house; the lighting feature suggests a flurry of leaves sweeping into the hallway.

MANHATTAN TOWN HOUSE

Upper East Side, New York, USA

This multilayered and characterful project in Manhattan evolved through a series of collaborations. Rabih Hage was commissioned by transatlantic clients whom he has known for many years, with the house representing the latest in a series of projects for the same family. Over time, Hage has developed a solid understanding of both the clients' interests on the one hand and also an appreciation of the way that the family like to live day to day. As well as working closely with the owners of the house, Hage also collaborated with the American architect Tom Kundig, of Olson Kundig, with the house representing a kind of dialogue between the two designers.

Kundig is best known for his imaginative rural houses, which are direct responses to extraordinary locations where an inventive approach to space and volume combines with a passion for strong, raw materials and textures, as well as industrial-style 'gizmos' such as winding wheels to open windows or sliding walls. The context here was clearly very different, with an existing red brick building from the late nineteenth century that had changed and evolved over time. A key role for Hage within the project was to soften the interiors and ensure that the house remained in tune with the requirements of the family and connected with their own sense of style and aesthetics.

'There was a creative tension, or dialectic, between a more industrial approach and the sense of warmth

that I wanted to introduce to make sure that the house felt homely', says Hage. 'So my job, really, was to ensure that the building feels welcoming and to soften the more industrial qualities of the project. In this respect, the conversation was very positive.'

The building is substantial and arranged over five main levels, plus a basement that houses a gym and service spaces; the rear of the property looks out onto a courtyard garden. Relatively few period features remained in the house, yet both Hage and Kundig wanted to ensure that the interiors still echoed the historical patina of the original building. This character comes through periodically - as seen in the arched windows that charmed the clients when they first saw them, or the feature walls of exposed bare brickwork.

A key element of the project was the creation of a central staircase that links the house together but also offers a sculptural centrepiece. The original staircase was effectively reinvented, with new timber treads and a sinuous plaster finish to the winding balustrade topped with a delicate bentwood banister. A skylight at the top of the staircase can be opened manually with a winding wheel manufactured by Turner Exhibits, and allows hot, stale air to vent upwards and outwards in the summer months; this skylight also draws natural light deep into the heart of the building.

A grand piano sits in front of an artwork by Ian McKeever to one side of the sitting room.

KERMIT'S DNA

LIGHT STRIP

The family lounge and
breakfast area sit to
one side of the kitchen;
the jungle artwork is by
Walton Ford, the nude
by John Currin and the
sofa by Antonio Citterio
for Flexform.

The master bedroom features walls covered in a Jim Thompson Thai silk with a period French chandelier.

The bunk beds in the children's bedroom are by Peggy Hlobil-Emmenegger; the chair is by Thonet.

Right, the children's den at the top of the house includes desks and work stations, with colourful chairs by Verner Panton and lights by Nacho Carbonell.

Far right, the boot room off the entrance hall has exposed brickwork and an eighteenth-century picture frame fitted with a mirror; there is space enough here to mount bicycles on the wall.

The ground-floor entry foyer leads past the stairway to a key family space. Here there is an open-plan lounge, dining/breakfast area and kitchen with a vast, pivoting wall of framed glass leading out to the terrace beyond. The American oak floors add texture and personality, and help to form an organic backdrop to an eclectic mix of furniture and art. The seating area is arranged around a custom-designed fireplace surrounded by bookshelves, which gives a library feel, while the sliding panel that can be used to separate this multifunctional space from the stairway doubles as a hanging space for art.

The breakfast area is positioned close to the pivoting window that leads out to the terrace, and is focused on a Piet Hein Eek dining table. The kitchen is to one side, dominated by a curvaceous, custom-designed island unit that offers a key focal point. Banks of timber-fronted storage cupboards are pushed against the wall, along with the cooking range and other appliances, arranged in neat, functional formation. Hage softened the space further with a dramatic ceramic chandelier by Ingo Maurer and a feature wall devoted to Piero Fornasetti's endearing Nuvole wallpaper with its calming cloud formations.

The floor above is devoted to more formal reception rooms, with a dining area and bar to the rear and a sitting room to the front, with space enough for a grand piano. Again, there are many layers to the interiors here. Soft grey Farrow & Ball colours form a foundation, combined with wooden floors, while a period stone fireplace from France helps to anchor the sitting room. Rugs, chandeliers

and a selection of contemporary, antique and mid-century furniture creates a blend that adds personality to the space in combination with the clients' art collection.

The dining room, similarly, features a curated mix of pieces with different provenances. A key element here is the dining table - or tables - by Terrence Woodgate and John Barnard, which can be divided into parts or combined for larger gatherings, creating a more flexible level of functionality. The dining chairs mix antique French pieces with mid-century classics.

The three floors at the top of the house offer bedrooms for the family of five, plus guests, while there is also a playroom and a 'common room' with desks for homework and study. The parents have one floor almost to themselves, with a master suite plus a separate study. 'The clients decided to have relatively small bedrooms but plenty of communal spaces', says Hage. 'So when the children are online or studying they are usually in one of these family spaces rather than locked away in a bedroom.

'Also, the family brought a lot of pieces with them from their previous home and we integrated them into the house, along with their art. So it gives the spaces more authenticity and gives the objects themselves a new life. It's really the opposite of disposable culture or disposable design. If you add up all of these things, you have a beautiful home that has a real meaning and purpose, combined with a quiet architectural approach defined by a conscientious attitude towards the building itself and its original character and patina.'

Two views of the
sculptural staircase, which
forms the backbone of
the house and also draws
in natural light from
a skylight above.

A view from the rear
courtyard of the informal
dining area and lounge,
alongside the kitchen; the
vast rear window pivots
to connect the inside and
outside spaces.

In the children's den
at the top of the house,
the large door in his
ubiquitous scrapwood
was commissioned from
Piet Hein Eek.

An eclectic assembly
of chairs, both antique
and modernist, surround
the carbon fibre dining
table. Right, an anteroom
alongside holds a bar.

Below and opposite, the concept drawing and realised space for the study featuring a ceiling light by Serge Mouille and custom shelving.

MAIN STUDY

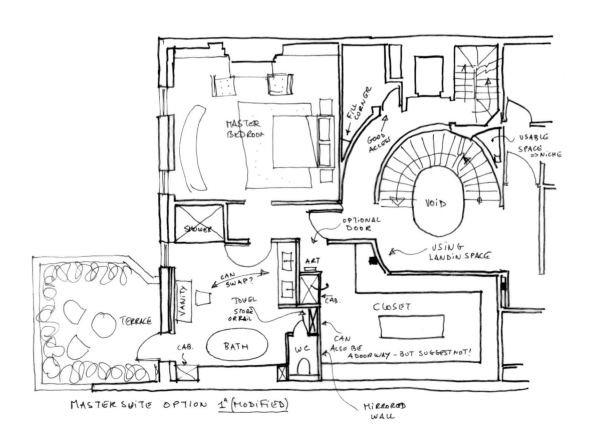

MASTER SUITE OPTION 1ᴬ (MODIFIED)

MASTER BATHROOM

Views of the marble master bathroom, with its sculptural bath tub.

The custom kitchen counter top, with a tap designed by Zaha Hadid and a backdrop of Piero Fornasetti Nuvole wallpaper.

THE
BOLTONS

South Kensington, London, UK

The oak panelled sitting room, with a photograph of the dome of the Theatine Church in Munich above the antique French fireplace; the chandelier is by Damien Langlois-Meurinne.

Many of Rabih Hage's clients seek him out because of his holistic approach to architecture and design. His atelier involves itself in all aspects of the design process, from structure and layouts through to the smallest interior details. This lends cohesion and unity to a project, which is a vital component of Hage's approach to quiet architecture. The owners of this family house in The Boltons approached his practice looking for a complete design concept that would encompass all aspects of the brief and embrace a series of substantial challenges.

'In many ways this is a typical project for us', says Hage, 'where we have everything from the concept to planning to completion, including the furniture and art. Here, the house was actually largely rebuilt but with respect for the external envelope above ground and the context of The Boltons. We have to link the house to its history rather than wiping out everything and starting again, but in this case there was not much to work with in terms of original features or elements. The most beautiful thing, before we started work, was the beautiful old tree in front of the house, which we kept of course.'

The house dates back to the 1860s and sits in The Boltons, a highly desirable Kensington enclave composed of two crescents and a communal garden. At some point, the house was carved up into two maisonettes and most of its period features were lost, including the fireplaces,

while the staircase was also damaged. The only clues that Hage was left with, apart from the façade, were some window shutters and some remnants of cornicing on the ground-floor level. As such, there was almost a blank canvas.

The clients wanted to turn the building back into a single-family house while also extending the available living space and introducing twenty-first-century amenities and services throughout. Hage adjusted the floor plates of the original residence where necessary, and converted the attic into an additional bedroom while also extending downwards to create three new levels. In total, there are now seven storeys, resolving a whole series of structural and technical issues.

Service spaces and subterranean lift-access parking were introduced at the lowest level. On the floor above this, Hage introduced a generously scaled swimming pool and spa, with skylights to one side drawing in natural light. There is a lounge feel to part of this space, with a seating area arranged around a fireplace plus a bar close by. There is, of course, a high level of luxury and sophistication here, but the space is also warm and welcoming, the textures of the stone floors and walls forming a backdrop to the fireside lounge.

The lower ground floor, which connects to the rear garden, is devoted to the kitchen and dining room, as well

as a bespoke and semi-transparent, glass-encased wine cellar that becomes a striking feature in itself. The dining room, although an evening space, draws in light from the garden outside and features a glass-topped dining table designed by Hage with, floating above it, a striking 24 Karat Blau chandelier - made up of gold leaf and acrylic Perspex plates - by Ingo Maurer.

The raised ground-floor level offers the house's main entrance and hallway, with the new staircase forming a grand feature in itself: an escalier balancé in stone with a French influence. The theme of transparency continues here with a series of custom-made, steel-framed glass partitions and sliding doors designed with an art deco flavour to them. These screens are both decorative and functional at one and the same time, creating a level of flexibility throughout the ground floor. In an open position, they allow free flow from the entrance hallway to the main reception room, which is a dramatic and welcoming space where natural light shines through from windows front and back, adding to the atmosphere of a space well suited to entertaining. Yet secondary screens in the same style can be drawn across to lightly partition the space as desired, creating more intimate zones for seating and relaxation; a separate study sits to the rear of the house on the same floor.

Here in the main sitting room, as elsewhere, services and storage are discreetly placed. Air-conditioning vents are invisible, while shelving and cupboards are hidden behind walls of veneered oak with hidden handles so that the wall surface remains flush and continuous. In this way, there is quiet luxury and practicality combined with warm textures and simplicity.

The same is true of the master suite, landings and bedrooms, where storage is tucked away behind bespoke walls with a detailing that is finely tuned and exquisitely crafted. Finishes such as the oak veener are repeated upstairs, adding to the sense of aesthetic cohesion, as you might see in a home from the Arts and Crafts period yet with a focus that is clearly contemporary in its purity.

'It's all about consistency and detailing', Hage says. 'Repeated materials help to make the home calm throughout, especially when you have inset handles and no visible hinges. We have hidden pegs, for instance, that pop out from the wall when you touch them so that you can hang your clothes but otherwise they are invisible. There's this uniformity to the design of these surfaces and details because I want everything to be calm. When you walk into these spaces you feel this sense of calm and rather than looking at the background you see the furniture, the objects, the art and the people within the space.'

Two section drawings
showing the basement
extension achieved by
underpinning the existing
building and also using
the piling technique.

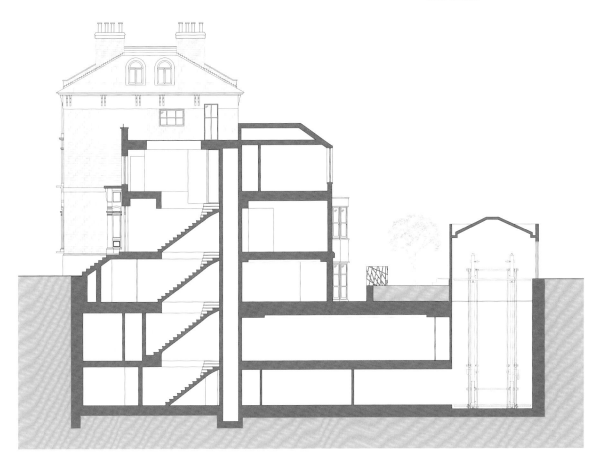

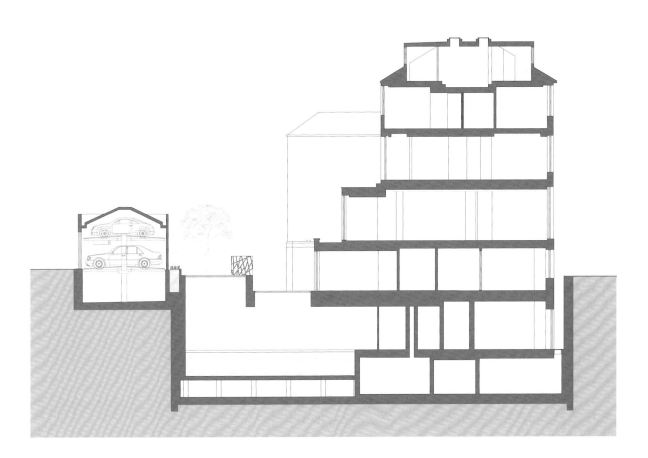

Hage designed a series of screens in glass and steel that lightly divide the hallway and sitting room, while also creating light partitions between different zones on the raised ground floor.

The master bathroom was created in a closet wing of the house and is flooded with natural light.

A dramatic chandelier
by Ochre and a fireplace
opposite the bed provide
key focal points, drama
and warmth in the
master bedroom.

Opposite, integrated
shelving and storage,
made in veneered oak
and antiqued bronze, sit
within the panelled walls
of the study; the desk is by
François Champsaur and
the metallic and marble
occasional tables are by
Jaime Hayon for Sé.

Oak and bronze kitchen details: bespoke kitchens are included in many of Rabih Hage's projects.

Oak panelled walls are used in many parts of the house, including the landing with its concealed lift door, adding texture but also creating a degree of cohesion characterised by precise and minimalist detailing. The alabaster wall light is by Pierre Chareau.

Natural materials such as the marble in the bathroom add pattern and character, the bespoke basin and vanity are in bleu de savoie marble.

While respecting the
period architecture of the
house, Hage extended
downwards to create
additional space and
re-landscaped the rear
garden (which now sits
above the new lower
floors), while introducing
lightwells that help
illuminate the lower levels.

KENSINGTON TOWN HOUSE

West Kensington, London, UK

Most residential projects require a degree of creative diplomacy, and particularly so when it comes to family homes. As well as conversations around context - with the aim of establishing a balance between updating a building for contemporary living and respecting the original character of a period property - there is generally a set of perspectives and outlooks within the family itself that needs to be considered. This was very much the case with this substantial home in West Kensington owned by a large family, with six children spanning a wide age range. Fortunately, Rabih Hage is a talented diplomat.

The clients had owned the Victorian property for a number of years by the time they approached Hage, who they selected partly on the basis of the way that he fuses architecture and interior design within a comprehensive approach. There was a need for more space for both entertaining and relaxation, but also a demand for quieter rooms and 'retreats'. The family has a strong interest in art and design, while both husband and wife had acquired a number of pieces of art and furniture from Asia during their travels. There was much to be done.

'As an architect and designer you are also an interpreter', says Hage. 'You are the catalyst for change, bringing technical knowledge on the one hand but also bringing the poetry that the clients are looking for in a project. It's all of these things. At the beginning I try to offer clients choices and options, because I want to see what they think and how they respond. I want them to be free to decide what's best for them rather than impose an aesthetic or dictate the functions of each space. There is a conversation and a process of moulding a house around the behaviour and living patterns of the family.'

The house overlooks a leafy garden square, with a private garden to the rear. Originally, the building was five storeys but Hage was able to secure permission to add an additional basement level, which created opportunities for new recreational and service spaces, including a home cinema, gym and wine cellar. There was also space for a semi-independent apartment for one of the older children. A roof terrace was added at the top of the building, and to one side Hage slotted in a new service zone with a lift that connects all levels.

There were also significant changes to the existing layout. The raised ground-floor level, in particular, was stripped back and reconfigured with a breakfast area placed in the bay window overlooking the garden square. This sits within the same overall space as the new and enlarged kitchen, which is in two parts. One part is more 'public', with an island unit doubling as a serving table or bar and bespoke cabinets sitting against a brick wall kept deliberately bare, with its raw textures contrasting with the restored cornicing. The second part consists of a more discreet service area to the rear, which can be used for preparation.

The lightbox installation in the sitting room is by Benjamin Faga, depicting the Arethusa Fountain at Bushy Park; the standing light is by Anton Alvarez.

Opposite and below, the combined kitchen and breakfast room contrasts exposed brickwork with more refined finishes for the island and storage units. The chandelier over the breakfast table is a vintage find from the 1970s.

A detail of the en suite master bathroom with a marble vanity unit and backdrop designed by Rabih Hage.

The panelled library
adopts a more masculine
aesthetic and features
pieces of furniture and art
collected by the clients
in Asia.

Left, the dining room with bespoke sideboard by Piet Hein Eek, Rabih Hage bucket dining chairs and an antique Japanese screen contrasting with the Victorian dining table.

Two views of the sitting room, including re-upholstered Queen Anne armchairs by the window and a photograph by Marilyn Minter. The central chandelier is by Jeff Zimmerman.

Left, the mirrored door in the ground floor hall leads to the glazed lift at the back of the house. Bespoke wall lights by Christophe Côme. Right, a view of the stairs at the second floor, with transparent glazed lift extension and artworks by Bai Yiluo.

Opposite, a chair and ottoman by Andrea Parisio for Meridiani in the master bedroom. The wall lights integrated within the curtains are by Serge Mouille.

The main sitting room sits on the *piano nobile* on the floor above. Benefiting from floor-to-ceiling windows and inviting proportions, the period elements of the space have been carefully restored or reinstated, including the cornices and moulded plaster ceilings. A bespoke Nepalese rug, floating upon the new herringbone floors, helps to define a central seating area, arranged around the fireplace, with a series of additional 'satellites' in other parts of the room. Each of these satellites is a composition in its own right, arranged around key pieces of furniture and art. The bespoke banquette against the wall opposite the fireplace, for instance, lies beneath a striking light-box photograph by Benjamin Faga with a sculptural brass table by the Haas Brothers sitting in front of it.

Other key spaces include the formal dining room, where the background offered by the walls, ceilings and floors is also soothing and calm. It creates a suitable foundation for more playful juxtapositions within the curation of the art and furniture - with, for instance, a period Japanese decorative panel hanging above a custom-designed sideboard by Piet Hein Eek. The library is more masculine in character, reflecting the interests of the husband of the house, with a melange of pieces from Asia and Scandinavia, as well as its bespoke bookcases.

Smaller spaces, such as cloakrooms and dressing rooms, are also highly crafted and beautifully detailed, while modern services - such as the lift - have been woven into the project with particular imagination. The stairway is now multilayered, with the original staircase tied to the new lift core on each level via a transparent screen of glass that allows the structural brickwork beyond this new addition to add another layer of texture. In this way, there is no attempt to hide the difference between old and new, with a vivid dialogue established between them.

'There is an element of "rough luxe"' to the exposed brickwork, here and in the kitchen, which just tones things down in terms of the luxury of the house and says we can be grand but we also know where we are coming from', explains Hage. 'These layers are about saying there is as much beauty in brick wall as the plastering or the cornicing. So why hide it? Let's keep it as part of the decoration because there is a truth to it that ties in with the real architecture of the building.'

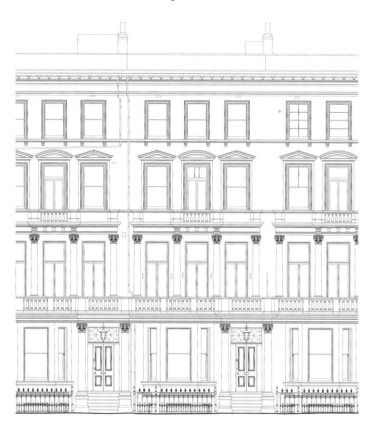

Opposite, elevation of
the front façade as it was
restored, with no sight lines
of the new stair access to the
roof terrace. Right and below,
views of the courtyard garden
to the rear and of the roof
terrace, with its hot tub.

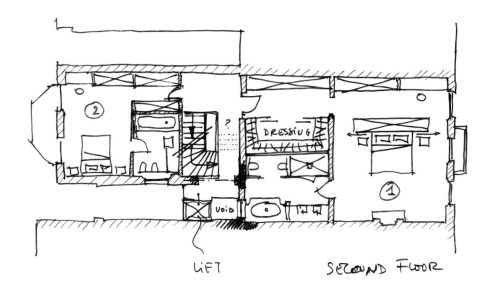

LIFT   SECOND FLOOR

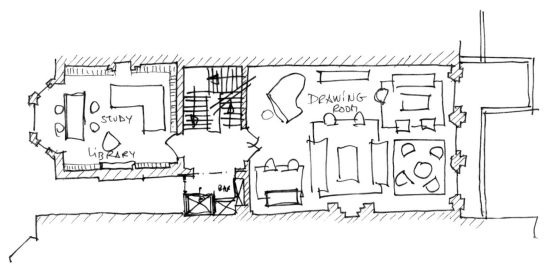

FIRST FLOOR

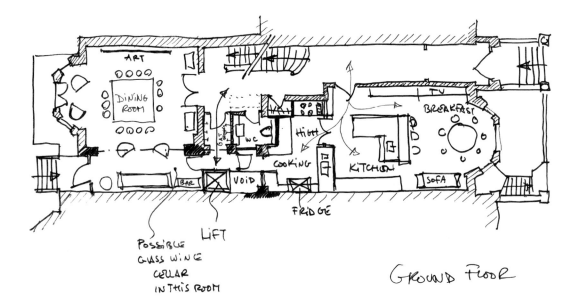

Studies for distribution
of the main floors.

GROUND FLOOR

ST JOHN'S TOWN HOUSE

St John's Wood, London, UK

Traditionally, the staircase has always been a key element that helps to define the identity of a town house. Within period homes in London, Paris or New York, the stairway is both a statement and a focal point with a crafted beauty and grandeur of its own. A grand, sculpted stairway helps to lift a house beyond the ordinary, and is lent extra gravitas by the apparent truth that it is usually one of the first features that we notice when we initially enter a house.

'The staircase is an important part of the journey of discovery as you enter a house and move through it', says Hage, 'but it also says a lot about who you are and the character of your home. Something that we often forget about, which is also important, is the tactility of the stairs. This is one of the elements that you really caress, even in a modern home, and it should feel special to the touch when you hold on to the banister.'

For Hage, the staircase is a crucial part of the town house, providing not just a functional backbone but a sculptural centrepiece. When he was commissioned to work on the interior architecture of a neo-Georgian home in North London, the design of the entrance hall and staircase became vital components in lending the house personality and establishing an invitation that draws you into and through the building with charm and interest.

The house is situated near Regent's Park, and was originally designed within the context of the area's neoclassical architecture. This provided the 'canvas', with Hage commissioned to create layouts and interiors over the four storeys of this grand, double-fronted building. Taking a degree of inspiration from the trees of the nearby park, Hage commissioned and co-designed a custom-made Lasvit chandelier for the entrance hall featuring an inviting flight of sculpted leaves that draw you inwards. The floor here features a modern variant on parquet, establishing a pathway that draws you through to the twists and turns of the escalier balancé with its sinuous walnut banister and solid limestone steps.

The hallway also carries you straight through to the main salon. This is a room partly defined by the luxury of space, with a central axis that continues onwards to a set of French windows that lead out into the back garden. To either side are two distinct seating areas, each arranged around the fireplaces that bookend the room while rugs floating on the stone floors help to both soften these zones and define them. The arrangement of these areas creates choices about how the room can be used, with the space ideally suited to entertaining but also allowing for more intimate moments and conversations, rather like a well-designed hotel lounge. A formal dining room nearby features a dining table that can easily seat a dozen, while a discreet, panelled wall holds both storage and

The drawing room, with elaborate coffered ceiling and cornicing which cleverly conceal the ventilation grills.

The sunken courtyard introduces light to the basement level but also provides a sculptural focal point for the family living spaces that surround it. The waterfall feature lends privacy to the glazed wall of the gym.

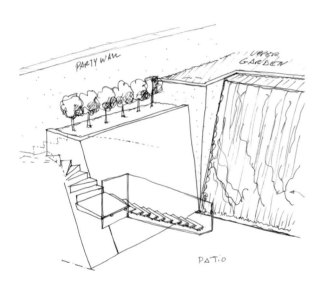

Opposite (far left), is one of two seating areas in the main sitting room, each one arranged around a fireplace; the coffee table is a Rabih Hage design.

Opposite (left), the dressing room with chandeliers by Patrice Gruffaz.

Opposite (far left), key spaces in the basement look out upon a swimming pool and sunken courtyard; the yellow 'Felt' chair is by Marc Newson and the coffee table by Carlo Contin for Meritalia.

Opposite (left), the bottom landing of the staircase, an area where the classic and contemporary elements of the house meet.

services, including access to a galley kitchen featuring a dumb waiter supplied by the principal kitchen on the floor below.

The master suite upstairs consists of a series of spaces, including his and her bathrooms and his and her dressing rooms. In this way, there is provision for a degree of privacy and independence, with the dressing rooms doubling as study spaces for catching up on work or correspondence. This allows the bedroom to retain a special status as a place of repose and relaxation. Within the master suite, as elsewhere, feature lighting by Patrice Gruffaz and other unexpected touches introduce

a more playful quality and lightly subvert the grown-up seriousness of the house in general.

The basement level of the house offers a dramatic contrast. Here, the focus is on a combination of family-friendly spaces and service areas with a more functional aspect to them. There is a high-spec kitchen and utility rooms on the one hand, and then luxuries such as a swimming pool and gym looking out onto a sunken courtyard on the other. There is also a family lounge and cinema room, with all of these more family-oriented areas contained within this distinct quarter of the home, set well apart from the more formal reception rooms upstairs.

Hotels. Architecture does not have to shout. It can whisper and still make a strong impact, with nuance and warmth.

– Rabih Hage

One of the guest
bedrooms at the Rough
Luxe Hotel in King's Cross.

As a guest, Rabih Hage prefers hotels with character and personality. Rather than opting for chain hotels, he prefers to seek out destination retreats that make him feel at home on the one hand yet also, on the other, reflect a sense of place and the surroundings. As an architect and designer he has adopted this approach when working on hotel concepts in various countries.

'For myself, I prefer hotels that feel like a real home with, for example, reception desks that don't feel like a reception desk when you walk in', he says. 'It's about feeling comfortable and welcome. With chain hotels the same ideas are repeated over and over again, wherever you are. I remember being in Sudan for a project and we were put in one of the chain hotels, which boasted that it was home from home because every room is always going to be the same anywhere you go in the world. But that's not what I want. I want to experience the Sudan or whatever the setting might be. You don't want to be parachuted into a style of design that is completely irrelevant to the location.'

Hage's view fits in with a sea change in attitudes towards hotels and increasing demand for retreats that are individual rather than repeat-pattern experiences. Whether in Berlin or Palamós, London or Finland, Hage looks to create conceptual designs that are also contextual designs. Each project becomes an adventure in itself.

'The context is the key to everything, and creating something that heightens your experience of a place rather than dulling it down', he explains. 'So each hotel has to be different and each location demands a fresh response and a building with its own style. If you are on safari then you might want to be in a tented hotel, and if you are in the mountains then perhaps a lodge or ski chalet. I want to be reminded of where I am rather than forgetting about it.'

One of Hage's first hotel projects was the Rough Luxe hotel in London's King's Cross. This was the first in a small group of individual and highly contextual hotels around the world. The King's Cross commission involved giving new life to an early Georgian town house in a rapidly evolving and dynamic neighbourhood. Yet it also involved creating a new concept for the group as a whole, drawing on the idea of character through texture - both physical and historical.

As Hage began working with the original building, it began to reveal its past via layers of paint and wallpaper, as well as period features that had survived through time. The more he uncovered, the more Hage wanted to keep and preserve this history and integrate it with his design approach. In many parts of the hotel, the aesthetic was driven by a combination of these carefully preserved textures working in combination with new elements and services, such as luxuriously appointed bathrooms. This was the beginning of a 'rough luxe' philosophy, which connects closely with Rabih Hage's ideas concerning 'quiet achitecture'.

'There is a humility and authenticity to the interiors along with these connections between the old and the new', says Hage. 'Rough luxe is an idea that goes beyond the hotels, of course, because it is a concept that also has wider relevance. As I talked about it, I realised that there are parallels with the Japanese wabi-sabi aesthetic, which also embraces the notion that there is beauty in imperfection. These ideas have resonance because we have moved beyond minimalism and the attempt to achieve perfection. Perfection is not beauty, because perfection can't last or perhaps does not exist at all. Minimalism is about having a perfectly polished surface or a beautifully painted and detailed wall. But then you knock it once and it's gone.'

This notion of beauty through imperfection overlaps with Hage's passion for furniture and interiors that embrace texture and provenance through recycling old materials, or upcycling and repurposing existing pieces. As well as often adopting such methods himself - within

his architecture, interiors and furniture design - Hage is repeatedly drawn to the work of designers with a similar ethos, such as artist Karen Ryan and designer Piet Hein Eek, whose tables sit within the courtyard at the Rough Luxe Hotel in King's Cross.

'When you look at the Rough Luxe or a piece of furniture by Piet Hein Eek, all these different layers that you see have a meaning to them', says Hage. 'Each time you look, you see something new and have a glimpse of another story. It's like design geology. You can look at these layers in different ways, like an artwork, and it becomes enriching. It's respecting the past and extending the life of materials, spaces and buildings.'

Following on from the Rough Luxe in King's Cross, Rabih Hage developed ideas for a number of other projects in very different settings that embraced a similar design philosophy. There was concept work for a beachfront hotel in the Spanish town of Palamós, for example, that revived and extended an existing building rather than sweeping it away - as some had suggested - and starting from scratch. Once more, the idea was to give the existing building a new life rather than demolishing it and starting all over again.

A rendering of the Versso hotel in Finland, which features a series of mirrored pavilions, reflecting the surrounding trees.

More recently, Hage was commissioned to create a completely new hotel in Finland. The Versso hotel project involves the design and construction of a substantial destination hotel on the island of Munapirtti, overlooking the Gulf of Finland. With its own spa, restaurant and other amenities, the hotel is a draw in itself but also connects with this rugged coastal landscape where the sea meets the forest. Versso aims to encourage tourism while seeking to preserve and protect the natural beauty of the surroundings. A key part of its offer is the outdoor experience - walking, cross-country skiing, sailing - and the allure of the spa and saunas, plus the temptations offered by the local produce and cuisine.

Given that this building represented a fresh start and a new experience, Hage was required to develop a narrative from the wider context of the surroundings rather than taking inspiration from an existing structure or building, as had been the case with Rough Luxe. With Versso, the key influence was nature itself while ensuring that the design of the building respects the natural surroundings and provides an immersive experience for guests, in which views of the trees and coast are always present.

While developing the design concept, Hage was also guided by the desire and necessity to create a sustainable building in every sense of the word. Versso makes use of sustainably sourced materials and also prefabrication techniques that maximise efficiency and reduce time on site. The hotel makes use of 'green' energy as well as local materials, labour and locally sourced fish, meat and other produce for its kitchens. The architecture of the building itself seeks to minimise the physical and visual impact of the hotel on such a sensitive site, using a coating of mirror glass that reflects the surroundings trees and thus camouflages the structure.

Versso is, therefore, in its own way, a 'quiet' building - yet one that is also rich in thought, ideas and stories. While Rough Luxe is tied into the urban history and fast-evolving character of King's Cross, Versso demands an opposite approach in which nature and the landscape become the driving imperatives. Yet both hotels offer, in their own way, a unique and individual experience that includes a level of luxury and sophistication. Hage's recognition of the importance of personality and individuality helps to set these projects apart.

Right, the reception lobby at the Radisson Edwardian Hotel in Guildford, where a crafted timber pavilion holds a more intimate waiting room.

Far right, the secret courtyard garden at the Rough Luxe Hotel provides an outdoor dining/breakfast room with tables and chairs by Piet Hein Eek.

ROUGH LUXE HOTEL

King's Cross, London, UK

The district of King's Cross has seen rapid and extraordinary change. This part of north London has recently been completely reinvented, transforming a quarter that was once neglected and shabby and turning it into a new and desirable urban 'village'. The area around the landmark stations of St Pancras and King's Cross is now home to new restaurants, homes, offices and cultural institutions, and buzzes with the energy and excitement that such regeneration brings with it.

During the first blossoming of new projects across King's Cross, Rabih Hage was approached by clients who had just acquired a Grade II listed building here, dating from the early 1830s, with the intention of opening a new hotel. It had originally been constructed as a large, single home and had already served time as a guest house over the course of its history. Some period features remained, and the building was layered with paint and wallpaper that echoed the complex story of the surrounding streets.

'The idea was to create a new hotel concept around this building, which was [to be] the first in a small group of hotels', says Hage. 'When I started looking at this building to see what was there, we began to take off some of the wallpaper to get a better idea and all these layers were revealed beneath with traces of older patterns and prints. So we decided that rather than stripping

everything away and re-doing it all, we would show the beauty of these layers and explore the story of the house itself with a minimum of structural changes. This was how the idea of Rough Luxe began.'

More recent partition walls were stripped away to reveal the true proportions of the late Georgian building. Fourteen former bedrooms were reduced down to nine in order to create more space for bathrooms and services, while Hage looked in detail at what could and should be preserved and what needed to be changed and updated. It was this contrast, or dialogue, between the new and the old that became a key part of the whole experience.

'Perfection doesn't mean beauty', he explains. 'What makes a hotel a great place to stay is the location, the welcome you get and how well you are looked after. Here, it was more important to keep the spirit of the house and create a place that would appeal to interesting and creative people.'

Fragments of period wallpapers and other textured surfaces were preserved and varnished. Modern services were introduced alongside them, including luxurious new bathrooms. In certain parts of the hotel, new wallpapers and photographic images used in the manner of trompe-l'oeil were introduced along with a striking collection of curated artworks, including a series of architectural photographs by Massimo Listri.

Contrasting textures are a key design element at the Rough Luxe; the photograph of Gilbert & George is by Jonathan Root and the chair is by Karen Ryan.

The eclectic blend of furniture echoes the multilayered character of King's Cross itself. There are bespoke elements, some antiques, a number of mid-century pieces and other items gathered at auction, including a collection of ceramics that once belonged to the Savoy Hotel. These elements of ironic playfulness feed into the identity of the hotel and the theme of faded grandeur. The notion of 'repurposing' also connects with a number of pieces by designers such as Patrice Gruffaz and Piet Hein Eek, with a series of the latter's dining tables specially commissioned for the hotel courtyard and made with reclaimed timber.

'The whole idea evolved into an experience – "the Rough Luxe Experience"', says Hage. 'It's all about the authenticity of the place and living in comfort but without excess ostentation. Everything in the hotel has a story to it that ties in with the design philosophy.'

The 'urban archaeology' behind this project helped to set it apart from chain hotels. A number of other Rough Luxe hotel projects followed in other parts of the world – including Switzerland, Spain and South Africa – all adopting a similar design ethos within characterful, period buildings. At the same time, of course, King's Cross continued to grow and evolve, and is now one of the most vibrant quarters in London.

In the bathrooms,
modern amenities and
contemporary finishes
contrast vividly with
the pattern and patina
of the original walls;
the photograph of
Philippe Starck is by
Jonathan Root.

The Rough Luxe provides
all of the modern
amenities and comforts
of a contemporary
hotel, while paying
respect to the history
and provenance of the
original building.

Playful touches punctuate the hotel throughout, creating a sense of individuality and character within each bedroom.

VERSSO

Munapirtti, Pyhtää, Finland

Guest bedrooms seek
a sense of connection
with the surrounding
landscape, while
introducing organic
textures and brighter
notes of colour.

Following on from the success of the concept and design work for the Rough Luxe hotel in London, Rabih Hage was approached to develop a fresh and innovative retreat in Finland. Supported by local government in the region, who wish to encourage eco-tourism, Versso is a new kind of hotel and spa that sits on a picturesque site on the island of Munapirtti within the municipality of Pyhtää. Located between Helsinki to the west and St Petersburg to the east, the island is relatively close to the Russian border and looks out over the Gulf of Finland. Connected to the mainland by a road bridge, Munapirtti is rural in character, with a handful of small villages but much in the way of rugged, natural beauty.

Hage was commissioned to design a substantial hotel here, with just over 100 bedrooms, while integrating the building into the landscape. Beyond this, a phased master plan also includes individual holiday homes and a marina, with substantial parts of the forested site and the coastline preserved and protected. Hage began with a number of trips to Munapirtti, seeking a better understanding of both the geographical and cultural context, with the island itself forming a powerful source of inspiration.

'A hotel with one hundred bedrooms is a large-scale project, so the challenge was all about how you integrate such a building into the landscape', says Hage. 'We didn't want to dig deep foundations or disturb the site any more than we had to, so the idea was to develop a series of inter-linked structures like a traditional, local fishermen's village in a modern form. But we also wanted to make the village disappear into the landscape, so we decided to make the modules reflective using mirrored stainless-steel cladding. The mirrors reflect the surrounding trees and the hotel starts to dissolve into the forest.'

The shape of the building has also been tailored to the topography of the site, as well as to the views across the Gulf. The central section of the hotel – which houses the spa, restaurant and communal areas – faces a modest promontory that pushes out into the water. The rows of interconnected structures that hold the guest bedrooms are arranged to either side, like curving birds' wings. This arrangement softens the outline of the hotel but also picks up on key sightlines and vistas, while ensuring a degree of privacy for the suites without the risk of them overlooking one another.

'The mirrored stainless steel coats these wooden, rectangular structures, which each have the individual scale of a fisherman's hut', Hage says. 'We decided to prefabricate these structures to save time and disturbance on site, so that we can then slot them into place next to one another. So the hotel becomes a mirage, reflecting the environment and the trees.'

The architectural approach is highly contextual, with the inter-connected pavilions looking to the sea but also interacting with the woodland surroundings.

The idea of discretion is key to the architecture of Versso, with the surface of the pavilions mirroring the trees, creating a subtle kind of camouflage within the landscape.

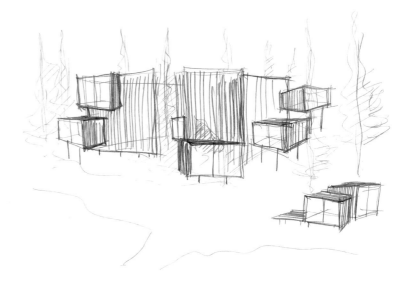

Prefabrication helps to enhance the sustainable aspects of the project, increasing the efficiency of construction, ensuring less waste and maximum thermal performance from the factory-made units. These super-insulated modules are largely made with sustainable timber and can be delivered by sea. The hotel also makes use of renewable energy sources, heat-recovery systems and rainwater harvesting.

For the interior finishes, Hage has drawn inspiration from both nature and the design traditions of the region, incorporating local materials and Nordic textures and patterns. The spa is a pivotal part of the whole project,

incorporating a range of different saunas as well as massage rooms, pools and relaxation spaces.

Many of the bedroom suites feature a private sauna, underlining the importance of this type of facility in this part of the world. The views are an essential part of these comfortable and escapist spaces, with picture windows plus window seats or lounge areas that connect with the outside. The rooms become observatories or belvederes, looking out into nature and the waters beyond. They serve as a kind of frame for appreciating the raw beauty of the winter months or the changing seasons.

The sense of transparency becomes more apparent in communal parts of the hotel such as the reception area, which is a clear glass box. Here, too, the indoor-outdoor connection is explored to the full. 'The idea was to create these spaces where you can connect with nature while feeling completely protected', Hage explains. 'It might be minus twenty outside in winter, but the view is always there.'

As well as using locally sourced materials, including timber and granite, Versso will also make the most of local produce in its restaurant and other parts of the hotel; two on-site smoke rooms will be used for curing fish and meat. Its approach to the surrounding landscape is governed by the need to conserve and protect nature while introducing walking trails and cycle paths, along with other invitations encouraging guests to step out and explore the island and the coast - including sailing, fishing and cross-country skiing.

'Versso is all about reflecting nature in every way', says Hage. 'It's a new build rather than using an existing building and the materials are new, but it's still a form of quiet architecture. The hotel respects its surroundings and connects with them while trying to disappear into the trees. At the same time, it is both luxurious and sustainable.'

The plan of the hotel was
developed around a series
of key sight lines and
vistas over the coast and
across the water.

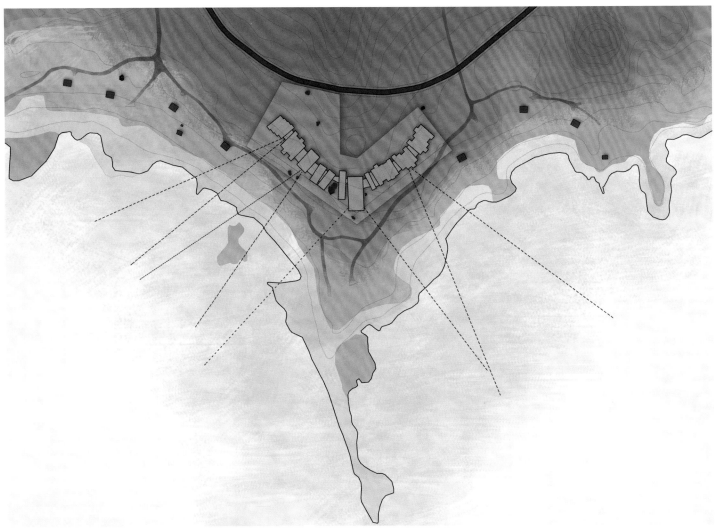

Right, the main
reception area plays
with themes of height,
scale and transparency.
Below, bedrooms
are both functional
and characterful.

RADISSON EDWARDIAN HOTEL

Guildford, Surrey, UK

While there is a growing appetite for hotels with personality and individuality, many hotel chains still prefer to create a brand identity and unified design approach that applies to many different kinds of buildings in many different contexts, countries and situations. Lending a branded chain hotel a level of individual character is, therefore, a challenge in itself. Following on from his work on the Rough Luxe concept in King's Cross, Hage was handed just such a commission with the design of the Radisson Edwardian Hotel in Guildford.

The building is part of a recently developed quarter in central Guildford that also includes the neighbouring G Live performance auditorium and arts centre, which seats 1000 people - some of whom are drawn to the hotel and its restaurants. The four-star Radisson has 185 bedrooms, as well as a spa, and sits on the site of an old coaching inn known as The White Horse. The hotel features a spacious, glass-fronted atrium that serves as its main entrance and reception area.

Given the vast scale and volume of this open space, which is the first part of the hotel that guests encounter, the task of crafting an inviting and welcoming reception zone was neither simple nor easy. Taking inspiration from the arts centre nearby, Hage turned the space into a kind of stage, picking up on some of the design language of the theatre with the use of lighting gantries and curtains.

'The idea is that every guest is a performer walking onto this stage', says Hage. 'The reception desks are hidden away to one side and quite subtle. They are almost hiding away, so that it does not feel like a hotel lobby in some respects. But at the same time, we also needed to introduce some warmth to the space and make sure that the "stage" was not too open or intimidating.'

This sense of warmth and welcome was introduced in a number of ways. Seeking to create several more intimate and reassuring retreats within the overall volume, Hage created a room within a room. This is a prefabricated, Macassar ebony box - with fitted, custom-made banquettes and a video installation of a fireplace by artist Benjamin Faga - that provides a shelter or waiting room. Like a crafted jewellery box, this room within a room offers a place in which to wait for a taxi or a friend without feeling exposed or on show. A staircase to one side of the box leads up to a kind of roof terrace, complete with fitted desks that provide a modest business centre, partially hidden away.

'When you are in this cube or cabana then you do feel more secure', explains Hage, 'but it also helps to humanise the whole space. The atrium shrinks down a little and the scale of it becomes less daunting.'

There are two other seating areas towards the back of the reception area, within part of the overall space

The design of the main reception areas seeks to balance the drama of open volumes with more intimate seating zones and break out spaces.

Below, a detail of one of
the seating areas within
the foyer, with lighting
designed by the Campana
Brothers.

but with a lower ceiling height. Here, Hage has created
custom-made banquettes against the walls plus additional
seating, along with statement lighting by Patrice Gruffaz
and the Campana Brothers, as well as diaphanous
curtains that lend these areas some sense of softness and
partial enclosure. Elsewhere in the atrium, Hage added
other artworks and super-sized theatrical elements,
rather like props on a stage. These include a vast, floating
crystal chandelier by Lasvit and a super-tall bookcase
against one wall, which picks up on the area's literary
connections - including links to Lewis Carroll, who spent
a good deal of time in the town. The surreal library ladder
that winds its way up the bookcase has the quality of an
Alice in Wonderland moment.

    Here, the context for the design approach was not
simply the building itself. In many ways, the existing
architecture presented problems and challenges that
needed to be overcome within an imaginative framework,
partly influenced by the theatrical and literary
connections within the neighbourhood. This cultural
context thus became a key driver for the project as a
whole, with the surrounding urban history and character
woven into the interiors of the hotel.

Within the triple-height atrium, Hage plays with scale to dramatic effect, introducing a super-sized chandelier and a triple-height bookcase.

Within the open lobby, the
waiting room is a private
and enveloping retreat; a
business station has been
installed upon its roof,
accessed by a side stair.

The triple-height bookcase and surrealist library ladder both pay homage to Lewis Carrol, who lived in Guildford for a time.

A large lenticular print of a
fire and a wall of artworks
offer another method for
bringing the height of the
atrium down to a more
human scale.

RELISH RESTAURANT

Radisson Edwardian Hotel, Guildford, Surrey, UK

As part of the interiors commission for the Radisson Edwardian in Guildford, Rabih Hage was tasked with the design of two new restaurant concepts for the four-star hotel. In some ways, these were experimental designs that looked to add a new aesthetic dimension within both the town of Guildford and the hotel group as a whole. But the restaurants also needed to connect with the design themes explored in the creation of the reception lobby and other public or communal spaces within the building.

The Relish restaurant, bar and lounge provides the flagship destination space in the hotel. It was designed to accommodate just over 180 covers and offer lunch and dinner, yet to come into its own principally during the evening. The restaurant's aesthetic ties in closely with some of the points of inspiration explored elsewhere in the hotel - especially the notion of the main reception area as a kind of stage, with a thematic link to the arts centre and auditorium nearby. This performance-space aspect tends to draw creative-minded people to the hotel and its amenities.

There is also the subtle influence of traditional French brasseries and cafés, which is expressed in the use of custom-designed banquettes and comfortable seating. Beyond this, the theatrical flourishes include Massimo Listri's striking photographs of colourful Italian palazzos

and other period buildings, which have some of the feel of stage scenery. Similar ideas are explored in pelmets that help soften and disguise the more functional-looking lighting tracks within the space, while diaphanous curtains invite connotations of the theatre on the one hand and also serve to soften the space and its acoustics on the other.

Chandeliers also provide drama, plus character, and work in combination with a wall of reclaimed and repurposed vintage mirrors. The contrasting forms and shapes of these mirrors and their frames add character and interest, but also generate a graphic quality. At the same time, the mirror glass has a somewhat dynamic aspect to it, helping to circulate light and movement through the space.

'The dimensions of the space itself were relatively large and wide', says Hage, 'so we worked with photography, fabrics and wallpaper to try and create a sense of depth and to warm the space in combination with the banquettes and the choice of furniture. The mirrors are all antique and the collection ties in with the idea of recycling or upcycling. Together, they are more than a sum of their parts and become a collection that adds character. Using a series of subtle touches and decorative elements I tried to introduce a feeling of serenity and a quiet but strong personality.'

Photomontages by Massimo Listri help introduce a sense of theatre, as well as notes of colour and character.

As well as
photomontages, wall
murals and artworks add
to the theatrical quality
of these spaces, which
are partially inspired by
the performance venue
alongside the hotel.

Murals and theatrical
lighting bring character
to the bar.

The theatrical theme carries through the restaurant and bar, with stage-style curtain detailing and feature lighting.

Another key part of the design approach to the restaurant was to create a variety of dining areas in addition to the banquettes, which sit alongside a series of square and rectangular tables. There is, for instance, an oval dining table near the bar and, further along, a circular table bordered with distinctive Mummy chairs (wrapped in elastic ribbon) by Peter Traag for Edra, with an antique chandelier floating above the table. Such fresh and fluid forms add special moments and prevent the restaurant from becoming too repetitive while also creating choice, with the larger tables particularly suited to groups or families. More than this, these shifts of rhythm introduce character through variety. In addition, Hage designed a separate VIP space and a more informal bistro - each with its own 'personality'.

CHRONOLOGY

1981
Moves from Beirut to Paris

1991
Graduates from the École des
Beaux-Arts, Paris-la-Seine, as
Architecte DPLG

1992
Joins the Arcora Group in Paris

1993
Establishes own architectural
partnership in Paris

2001
Launches an eponymous atelier
in London

2004
Awarded Interior Designer of
the Year by IdFX Magazine

2005
Palace Gate, Kensington,
London, UK

2007
Holland Park Residence, London,
UK

2008
Rough Luxe Hotel, King's Cross,
London, UK

Establishes DeTnk, an online
think tank dedicated to
collectible design

2009
Prince's Gate Court,
South Kensington, London, UK

Wins European Hotel Design
Award (Innovation Award)

2010
The Old Rectory, Oxfordshire, UK

2011
Paris Apartment, Trocadéro,
Paris, France

Holiday Home, Cotswolds, UK

Awarded the Andrew Martin
International Interior Design
Award

2012
The Pool House, Oxfordshire, UK

Radisson Edwardian Hotel,
Guildford, Surrey, UK

Awarded the Chevalier de l'ordre
national du Mérite and *Homes &
Gardens* award for Interior Design

2013
Mews House, Chelsea, London,
UK

2014
Kensington Town House,
West Kensington, London, UK

2015
Manhattan Town House,
Upper East Side, New York, USA

St John's Town House,
St John's Wood, London, UK

2016
Hage establishes a satellite office
in New York

The Boltons, South Kensington,
London, UK

Carlow House, Camden, London,
UK

Maison Luberon, Provence, France

2017
The Chilterns, London, UK

Beirut Penthouse, Beirut, Lebanon

2017–2020
Versso Hotel, Munapirtti Island,
Finland

2018
Transitional Housing Concept,
London, UK

ACKNOWLEDGEMENTS

I would like to express my immense gratitude to the people who have
given me their support, believed in me and my work and have been
and remain a great inspiration. In particular: Kurt & Carmen Engelhorn,
James & Kathryn Murdoch, Stephen Conway, Teena & Jakob Stott,
William Collins, Judy Dobias, Françoise Sarré, Elizabeth & Carl Azar,
Terence Cole, Mark Steinberg, Lindsey Behrens, Tobias Elbl, Rima
& Kamal Jabre, Susan Crewe, Liz Elliot, Lucia van der Post, Matthew
Croxford, Benoit Faure-Jarrosson, John & Kathleen Buck, Michael Hsu,
Maria & Malek Sukkar, Rima Shehadeh, Mireille Masri, Françoise de
Pfyffer, Sheikhas Fajer & Feryal Al-Sabah, Lani Martin & Joel Van Dusen,
Edith Mézard and Charles Burdick.
      And a huge thank you to the reliable, creative and always consistent
members of my team, past and present, without whom the projects
would not happen, in particular: Irene Capote, Chloë Østmo, Michelle
Silver, Natalia Stawecki, Lucinda Readhead, Camilla Corbett, Sandra
Romberg, Rosie Spendlove, Guita Gharebaghi and Ed Behrens.
I would like to thank Dominic Bradbury, Amanda Kasper, Laura
Colonnese, Val Rose, Sarah Thorowgood and all the team at Lund
Humphries for making this beautiful book happen.
      Finally I would like to express my deepest gratitude to the people
who consistently motivate me to make things better; my family: Ghada,
William and Charlotte.

Rabih Hage, 2018